GO GREEN
SAVE MONEY

AA

First published 2009
Produced by AA Publishing
© AA Media Limited 2009

ISBN 978-0-7495-6160-4

Published by AA Publishing (a trading name of AA Media Limited, whose registered office is Fanum House, Basing View, Basingstoke, Hampshire RG21 4EA; registered number 06112600).

Visit AA Publishing at www.theAA.com/bookshop

A03980

A CIP catalogue record for this book is available from the British Library.

The contents of this book are believed correct at the time of printing. Nevertheless, the publishers cannot be held responsible for any errors or omissions or for changes in the details given in this book or for the consequences of any reliance on the information it provides. This does not affect your statutory rights. We have tried to ensure accuracy in this book, but things do change and we would be grateful if readers would advise us of any inaccuracies they may encounter.

Every effort has been made to credit all sources used. If we have inadvertently omitted any acknowledgements, we will be happy to make any necessary arrangements at the following reprint.

Written by Finny Fox-Davies and Kim Davies
Senior Editor: Penny Fowler
Layout and Design: Tracey Butler
Internal Repro & Image Manipulation: Sarah Montgomery
Picture Researcher: Liz Stacey
Proof Reader: Barry Gage

Commissioning Editor: David Popey

Repro by Keenes Group, Andover
Printed by Rotolito Lombarda SPA, Milan, Italy
(FSC, ISO 9001:2000 and SMETA accredited.)

We would like to thank the following for reviewing pages of the book as given:
Energy Saving Trust, pages 8–25, 26–33, 36–41, 46–49.
Association for Organics Recycling, pages 34–35.
AA Technical Specialist, Vanessa Guyll, pages 42–45.
Ethical Consumer Research Association, pages 50–67, 82–93.
Women's Environmental Network, pages 68–93.

Cover photos:
RecycleNow Partners Photo Library (left and centre);
© David R. Frazier Photolibrary, Inc./Alamy (right)

Mixed Sources
Product group from well-managed forests and other controlled sources
www.fsc.org Cert no. SW-COC-002295
© 1996 Forest Stewardship Council

Pages 6–7 (from left to right): Paper is generally collected from our doorstep so there's no excuse for not recycling.(L)

Following the four Rs can reduce the amount of material going into landfill. (C) Clothes can be recycled in a clothing bank

or taken to a charity shop. (R)

GO GREEN
SAVE MONEY

FINNY FOX-DAVIES & KIM DAVIES

CONTENTS

THE FOUR Rs
(REDUCE, REUSE, REPAIR, RECYCLE)

Environmental awareness is an increasing part of our lives but many people still do not fully realise the difference that they, as individuals, can make. The energy consumption of millions of homes is having just as much environmental impact as heavy industry, so it is the responsibility of all of us to adopt energy-saving methods to safeguard the health of the planet.

Go Green Save Money provides practical and sensible guidance to help you to save energy and money at the same time. Going green isn't difficult and by adopting the four Rs, it soon becomes second-nature.

Reduce

Reducing our energy consumption can be achieved in many different ways – using energy-efficient appliances and low-energy light bulbs, insulating our homes and turning down the heating, walking to the shops instead of driving or taking the train not the plane – these measures aren't difficult, don't cost a lot and they can save a great deal.

Perhaps the easiest way to save money and look after the planet is simply to reduce the amount of stuff we buy. Imported goods are so cheap that we often replace appliances without a second thought. This may be a small cost to us but manufacture

and transit pollute and discarded appliances add to landfill sites.

Reuse

We could get more use out of many of the things we throw away – T-shirts can be reused as cleaning cloths and sofas recovered instead of replaced. Reusing the T-shirt saves us buying cleaning cloths or kitchen towels, which take energy to manufacture and transport – and when we've finished with the T-shirt for cleaning, it can still be recycled for fibre or composted.

Many items made from recycled goods are also now available to buy, helping to keep the cycle going.

Repair

Taking a long-term view when buying manufactured goods can save money as well as reducing CO_2 and landfill. Buying well-made goods in the first place means they will last longer and when they do go wrong they are more likely to be repairable. Adopting a 'fix-it' approach can save on all levels. Furniture that is damaged can be repaired and carpets can be professionally cleaned. Repairs don't even have to be professional – a tube of glue will often mean you can go on using that favourite mug.

Recycle

Landfill is full to bursting and a lot of it will take centuries to decompose. The average British household puts out half a tonne of rubbish each year, more than half of which need not be there. Adjusting our daily habits and rethinking our 'disposable living' culture will make a difference. Commercial recycling is increasing all the time and local authorities make it easy for us by collecting paper, glass, cans and plastic from our doorstep.

THE GREEN HOME

There are many ways to introduce and practise an eco-friendly lifestyle but as our home is where we create the most CO_2 emissions, it is the best place to start. Changes don't have to be radical and every little adjustment will make a collective difference, saving us pounds and reducing CO_2 emissions. Being more aware of the materials we use in our homes will also reduce the number of artificial chemicals in our surroundings so our health can benefit too. The following suggestions for creating a green home will save money and improve your quality of life, in both the short and long term.

Left: With government grants available, it may be an option to generate your own renewable energy.

ENERGY EFFICIENCY

Overall, domestic energy consumption in the UK has gone up by a third since 1970, so houses are making a bigger contribution than ever to global warming. By taking steps to make our homes more energy efficient, we can cut back our energy costs and reduce our carbon footprint.

Take stock

Assessing your current energy usage is the first step towards saving energy and money.

- **Carbon footprint assessment** – Will highlight where you can make changes (see *http://actonco2.direct.gov.uk).*
- **Wireless electricity monitors** – Available from high street electrical and department stores from £30, these handy devices monitor the energy usage of your electrical appliances. The result is to send you running to switch appliances off, resulting in a self-imposed drop in electricity usage.

Shop around for your energy

The various energy suppliers are very competitive and switching can save pounds off your annual bill (see *www.uSwitch.com).* Alternatively, switch to a green energy supplier (see *www.greenelectricity.org).*

HOME INFORMATION PACK (HIP)

Energy efficiency assessment has become a legal requirement for house sales and rented accommodation and will no doubt make a difference to the value of a property. Apply the same efficiency measures to save on energy costs day-to-day. Rated between A and G, the lower G rating is given to:

- No heating controls
- Inefficient and oil central-heating boilers
- Draughty floors, doors and windows
- Insufficient or no insulation.

Central heating

Central-heating boilers are responsible for around 60 per cent of both CO_2 emissions in an average gas-heated home and your annual fuel bill.

- **Replace your boiler** – If your boiler is inefficient and certainly if it's 15 years old, replacing it with an A-rated energy efficient condensing boiler which incorporates an extra heat exchanger could save around a third of your heating costs.
- **Rate your boiler** – See *www.boilers.org.uk* to find out how efficient your boiler is.
- **Boiler settings** – Get to grips with your heating controls and fine tune settings for greater efficiency.

Renewable energy

Most of our energy comes from fossil fuels (coal, gas, oil). These fast-diminishing resources are non-renewable, expensive to generate and a major source of CO_2 emissions. However, there are a number of grant-aided renewable energy options for individual homes that generate free energy with no CO_2 emissions (see *www.energysavingtrust.org.uk/grantsandoffers*).

- **Wind power** – Small-scale wind turbines can be attached to the house or a mast erected in the garden. Installation costs are from £1,500 and savings will depend heavily on location and local wind speed.

- **Solar power** – A well-placed water-heating panel can provide 30 per cent of the annual hot water requirement of a three-bedroom house. Photovoltaic panels convert daylight into electricity. They're more expensive to install but you can store surplus electricity or sell it via your energy supplier.

- **Ground source heat pumps** – Consider installing if you are doing landscaping. They take advantage of the constant higher temperatures below ground level. Energy savings depend on the extent of the installation but the potential is more than 50 per cent of your annual energy costs.

Did you know...?

If everyone in the UK with gas central heating installed a high-efficiency condensing boiler, it would save enough energy to heat 3.4 million homes for a whole year.

Source: The Energy Saving Trust

- **Biomass** – Room heating wood-burning stoves are categorised as carbon neutral, are cheap to run and reduce the demand on your central heating. A biomass central-heating boiler replaces your gas or oil central-heating boiler, supplying heating and hot water. It burns wood pellets or chips via an automatic feeder so you only have to refill it every few days.

Right: Wind is currently the world's fastest growing renewable energy source.

INSULATING YOUR HOME

Unless they are newly-built or super energy-efficient, homes waste hundreds of pounds worth of heat every year. An average UK household creates around six tonnes of carbon dioxide a year – that's double the average annual carbon dioxide emissions of a car. Insulation is the key factor in reducing our energy costs and carbon footprint.

Why insulate?

An uninsulated house could be losing 60 per cent of the heat it generates through its roof and walls.

- **Grants** – Grants to help with the cost of roof and wall insulation are available to all households. (For more information see *www.energysavingtrust.org.uk/ grantsandoffers*).
- **Ventilation** – Don't forget that maintaining adequate ventilation is important in order to avoid condensation.

£ *Cavity-wall insulation*
At current prices cavity-wall insulation could cut your energy bill by around £160 per year.
Source: The Energy Saving Trust

Start at the top

The roof is one of the biggest sources of heat loss. Fitting loft insulation is an easy and cost-effective way to save energy.

- **DIY** – A weekend job requiring care and common sense and costing about £300.
- **Professional** – Costs around £500.

Wrap-around warmth

External walls lose about 30 per cent of the energy used to heat our homes. Most brick houses constructed after the 1920s have an inner and outer wall with an air-gap between them that can be filled with cavity insulation. Solid walls lose even more heat than cavity walls and are more expensive to remedy but the long term savings are greater and outweigh the initial cost.

- **Cavity insulation** – It takes just two to three hours to pump insulation material into the wall cavity of a three-bedroomed, semi-detached house. Usually done by a contractor for about £500, it will take about two years to recover installation costs.
- **Internal insulation** – This is the cheaper solution for solid walls at around £42 per sq m (£4 per sq ft) and a current average saving of £470 per year. It will reduce your living space by about 90mm (3.5in).

Did you know...?

Going from no loft insulation to the recommended 270mm (10in) cuts your carbon emissions by around one tonne and your heating bill by around £205 per year.

Source: The Energy Saving Trust

- **External insulation** – This is fixed to the outside wall and covered with a decorative finish or cladding. Average installation cost is £5,600 and the heating bill saving is around £500 per year.

Door, floors and windows

Draughts account for a smaller percentage of heat loss from our homes but they cause the greatest discomfort and encourage us to turn up the heating. Replacement double glazing is the best solution for badly fitting windows; but there are many cheap, simple and effective measures for cutting draughts around windows, doors and floors.

- **Draught excluders** – Self-adhesive draught excluders around windows and doors are an easy first step. Fit brush draught excluders across the bottom of the door and over the letterbox.

- **Seal gaps** – Check for gaps between the window frame and wall and, around skirting boards and floors.
- **Secondary glazing panels** – These are available from leading DIY stores. They fit on the inside and are an alternative to sealed unit double-glazed windows.
- **Floor insulation** – Cut heat loss through wooden floors by insulating below and between the joists. Make sure not to block the airbricks. Concrete floors can be covered with sheet insulation.

Hot water

Hot-water pipes and cylinders are another source of heat loss that is easy and inexpensive to remedy.

- **Hot-water tank** – If the air space around your hot-water tank is nicely warm and cosy, it is losing you money. You can stop this by fitting a thick insulating jacket. It will cost you around £12, save you around £40 per year and cut your annual carbon footprint by about 195kg.
- **Pipe insulation** – This can be very easily fitted over exposed pipes. It will cost around £10, save around £10 per year and cut carbon emissions by approximately 65kg per year.

Above: Insulation can be made from natural substances such as sheep's wool.

REDUCING HOME ENERGY USE

Most homes have a host of gadgets and appliances which collectively use a huge amount of electricity and release equally huge amounts of CO_2 emissions. With a little thought we can make our energy guzzlers work better for us and seriously reduce our home energy consumption and costs.

TOP 30 TIPS

Around the home

1. Invest in a wireless electricity monitor.
2. Never leave appliances on standby – this accounts for 8 per cent of household electricity use.
3. Replace light bulbs with low energy bulbs – average annual saving is £3 per bulb.
4. Turn lights off when you leave the room.

Living room

5. Close the curtains at dusk to keep in heat.
6. Choose the smallest screen TV for your needs. Small TVs use far less energy than large screen ones.
7. Use multi-function electronics such as a combined TV and set-top box.
8. Don't leave chargers plugged in.
9. When you need to upgrade your computer, choose a laptop, they cost about 85 per cent less to run.
10. Turn off the printer, it is still using energy even when it's idle.

Kitchen

11. Don't boil more water than you need.
12. Fit a SAVAplug or similar device to cut your fridge's energy.
13. Don't put warm food in the fridge – it takes a lot more energy to cool it down.
14. Choose electrical appliances of the best quality and energy efficiency you can afford, it will be cheaper in the long run.
15. Don't run the tap when washing-up.

Bathroom

16. Turn the water thermostat down to 60°C (140°F).
17. Run a basin of hot water for shaving.
18. Fit an aerated shower head, it works by adding air to the water so you use less.

Did you know...?

Leaving the tap running while you brush your teeth uses on average six litres of water a minute.

Source: The Energy Saving Trust

10

Heating

19. Turn your heating thermostat down by one degree celsius and save around £65 a year on heating costs.

20. Rather than automatically turning the heating on in winter, think about wearing warmer clothes instead.

21. Check your loft insulation and if necessary top it up to the recommended 270mm (10in) for an easy way to conserve heat.

22. Make sure all external doors have a draught excluder and seal gaps around windows, skirting boards and floors.

23. Check your heating is only on when you need it.

24. Upgrade your central heating controls and fine-tune the heating levels for maximum efficiency.

25. Invest in thermostatic valves for your radiators.

26. Fit heat reflectors behind the radiators.

27. Turn down or switch off the radiator in the spare room using a thermostatic radiator valve (TRV).

20

Bedroom

28. Check your bedroom temperature – the ideal is around 18°C (65°F).

29. Switch off the electric blanket and use a hot-water bottle.

30. Get a wind-up or battery alarm clock.

THE GREENER KITCHEN

Kitchen appliances account for nearly half our electricity use and very often they are horribly inefficient in their energy consumption. Changing appliances to A-rated and A+ or A++ models will cut CO_2 emissions as well as your electricity and water bills.

Low-energy cooking

Cooking uses a lot of energy (up to 8 per cent of domestic electricity consumption) but there are ways to make the most of that energy. There are also alternatives to using a gas or electric cooker that will speed up cooking times and make life much simpler.

- **Pressure cooker** – A worthwhile investment for the kitchen. It considerably reduces cooking times.
- **Microwave** – Cooking certain foods in the microwave can reduce the energy needed by between 20 and 80 per cent – and cooking often takes a fraction of the time.
- **3-tier saucepan stack** – Use this to cook three different foods on one ring.
- **Saucepan lids** – Put a lid on a boiling saucepan and cut down the cooking time. When cooking pasta or rice, bring it to the boil, cover with a tight-fitting lid, turn off the heat and leave it to cook for the usual time.

A-RATED COST SAVINGS

All new appliances must show their energy rating between A and G. The difference in the annual energy consumption can make a dramatic difference to the annual running cost.

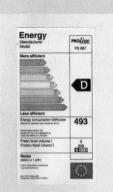

Washing machine (five washes per week):
A – £30; B – £30; C – £32; D – £39; E – £42; F – £46; G – £49

Tumble dryer (three washes per week):
A – £50; B – £58; C – £65; D – £73; E – £81; F – £89

Fridge-freezer:
A++ – £23; A+ – £33; A – £45; B – £53; C – £67

Dishwasher (five washes per week):
A – £44; B – £49; C – £57; D – £64; E – £66

Source: The Energy Saving Trust

Kitchen furniture

The majority of fitted kitchens are constructed from plastic laminates and foils wrapped around particle and composite board. The manufacturing process gives off high levels of CO_2 and these materials continue to give off gas once the cupboards are fitted (see pages 22–23, *The Healthy Home*). These fitted kitchens are not particularly hard-wearing and between wear-and-tear and fashion choices they are replaced frequently at great cost to the environment and your pocket.

- **Recycle natural wood furniture** – Quality wooden furniture can be reused as free-standing kitchen fittings.
- **Invest in quality** – Consider how many times you might refit your kitchen and invest in having fitted cupboards built from wood. They will last much longer and you can always update them with different paint finishes or replacement cupboard doors.

Did you know...?

If everybody boiled only the water they needed for their cup of tea, the power saved could supply electricity to 300,000 homes.
Source: The Energy Saving Trust

SIMPLE MEASURES

There are many small measures that can make a difference to your carbon footprint as well as saving you money.

- Compost your kitchen peelings.
- Match your pan to cooker ring size.
- Avoid using cling film; wrap food in greaseproof paper, put a plate over a bowl of food or use recyclable food storage containers.
- Don't open the fridge or a heated oven more often than you have to – it will have to work hard to counteract the change in temperature.
- Use a cotton cloth instead of kitchen paper but if you do use kitchen paper, add it to the compost bin.
- Don't waste oven space, plan meals to make full use of heated ovens.

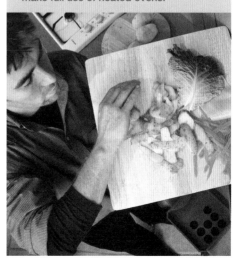

WATER USE AND LAUNDRY

According to Waterwise, most households drink only about four per cent of their daily water consumption. The rest goes down the drain or onto the garden. Meanwhile, the average British household gets through around 17,000 litres of water and produces CO_2 emissions of 120kg a year just doing the laundry. Save water, energy and money with these simple measures.

Conserving water

Providing pure drinking water to every home in Britain is an expensive process that consumes a lot of energy. Reducing consumption will cut your water bill and conserve water supplies. Making sure we don't waste water is the first step.

- **Leaking taps** – A dripping tap could waste up to 5,500 litres of water a year and cost up to £18 a year if you're on a water meter.
- **Flow restrictors** – Your tap delivers water at up to 20 litres a minute. Fit a 'flow restrictor' or 'spray head' to reduce flow.
- **Turn off taps** – Don't run the tap while cleaning your teeth.
- **Use a bowl** – Rinse vegetables, dishes and handwashing in a bowl of water and not under a running tap.

- **Toilet cistern** – Fit a modern low or dual-flush toilet cistern, or add a cistern displacement device such as a 'hippo' or a 'save a flush' bag. A homemade alternative is to fill a two litre container with water.

Recycle water

A lot of the water that goes straight down the drain could be diverted and used for other household tasks.

- **Bathwater** – There is no need for every member of a family to have fresh bathwater – time your baths to share water.
- **Washing machine hosepipe** – This can be diverted into a bucket. The soapy water can be used to clean windows, wash floors or clean the car.
- **Vegetable cooking water** – Allow to cool and then pour on house or garden plants – all those nutrients will do them good.

Doing the wash

The average Biritish household uses the washing machine five times a week. Adjusting how we get through the weekly laundry will cut down the work and reduce the energy needed, as well as the cost.

- **Wait for a full load** – Two half-loads use more energy and water than a full-load.

A useful system is to keep three laundry baskets for light colours, dark colours and whites – you can see at a glance when it's time to run a wash cycle.

- **Turn it down** – A 30°C wash uses 40 per cent less energy than washing at higher temperatures and gets most things clean.
- **Washing detergents** – Cut out bleaching agents and corrosive substances by using non-toxic, biodegradable detergents.

£ Time to upgrade

Replacing your old washing machine with an Energy Saving Recommended one (look for the energy saving label, below left) could save you up to £11 a year.

Source: The Energy Saving Trust

Drying your clothes

An ordinary washing line is the most eco-friendly way to dry your clothes and it's free.

- **Less tumble drying** – Line dry for the summer months and reduce your drying bill by around £16 a year.
- **If you must tumble dry** – Run full-loads, dry similar fabrics together and clean out the lint filter for greater efficiency.

Ironing

Ironing is yet another drain on your electricity supply and another source of carbon emissions so it's worth thinking about how you can cut down and save on ironing.

- **Don't use the steam function** – Iron clothes while they are still a little damp or use a plant sprayer – the steam function takes more energy to heat up the water.
- **Switch off** – Turn the iron off before pressing the last item – it will still be hot enough to use.
- **Think before you iron** – Can you just fold the items instead?

Right: A bit of thought can make your ironing more energy efficient.

GREEN CLEANING

Look along the supermarket shelves and there seems to be a cleaning product for every task imaginable – and most of them contain chemicals that are classed as hazardous waste. With the best of intentions we are covering our homes with toxic chemicals that may cause headaches, irritability and lack of concentration.

Supermarket alternatives

Most supermarkets now sell a selection of eco-friendly cleaning products, including own-brand ranges. Covering most household cleaning requirements, they vary in cost and efficiency but compare well with chemically based products.

- **Ingredients** – These are mostly plant-based with no toxic chemicals.
- **Packaging** – This may be refillable, made from recycled materials, recyclable – or all three of these.

Did you know...?
Manufacturers of household cleaning products are not legally obliged to test them for safety or to state the ingredients on the product.

Natural cleaning solutions

You can clean the house just as well without using any manufactured products. The cost is a fraction and there is no risk of health hazards and water pollution. Essential oils such as lavender, rosemary and tea tree oil can be added to homemade cleaning mixes to add anti-bacterial and anti-fungal properties, as well as making the cleaning solutions smell good.

- **Bicarbonate of soda** – This is an effective deodoriser, stain remover, water softener and metal polisher. Sprinkle onto carpets and leave for 15 minutes to clean and deodorise – this is good for pet odour. It is available online or from a pharmacy for around £2.75 per kg (£1.25 per lb). Also useful for making cleaning solution mixes.

Above: Bicarbonate of soda and lemon juice can both be used as stain removers

- **Soda crystals** – Washing soda is available from supermarkets and hardware shops. It is a useful ingredient for general purpose cleaning and laundry. It can irritate the skin so is best used wearing rubber gloves.
- **Lemon** – The citric acid in lemons will remove stains, improve laundry, deodorise, remove limescale and clean brass and copper. Add lemon juice to your laundry wash and line dry it to make the whites and colours brighter and fresher.
- **Vinegar** – White vinegar has a milder smell than malt vinegar but both will disinfect, clean stains, remove mildew, grease and wax polish build-up. To achieve smear-free windows and mirrors, spray vinegar and water onto the glass and clean off with scrunched-up newspaper.
- **Salt** – Mix with an equal amount of plain flour, add vinegar to make a paste – good for cleaning surfaces, especially metals.
- **Olive oil** – Used sparingly, can clean stainless steel and leather and polish wood.
- **Soapnuts** – Available online from *www.gogreen.cellande.co.uk* or other eco-friendly stores, these contain saponin, a natural detergent. Two or three in a washbag, can be used in the washing machine for several washes and will produce good results at low temperatures. Also useful for general cleaning and can eventually be composted.
- **Pure soap** – Dissolved plant-based soaps are an essential addition to the cleaning solutions ingredients. A good tip is to buy good petroleum-free soap for the bathroom and when it becomes less inviting to use, dissolve the bar in hot water to make liquid soap. Alternatively, buy pure soap flakes and dissolve them in hot water.

Cleaning solutions mixes

Use natural ingredients to mix up your own cleaning solutions.

- **Washing-up liquid** – Equal parts of soap flakes with bicarbonate of soda, add water.
- **Dishwasher powder** – Two tablespoons each of bicarb and borax, add vinegar to the rinse-aid dispenser.
- **All purpose cleaner** – One teaspoon each of soda crystals and liquid soap, two teaspoons of borax and 250ml (0.5 pint) hot water. Put ingredients in a spray bottle and add hot water to dissolve.
- **Anti-bacterial solution** – Half water and half hydrogen peroxide (from a chemist). Use from spray bottle to destroy bacteria including salmonella and E coli.

THE HEALTHY HOME

Almost everything for the home is available in synthetic materials, many of which may give off toxic gases. This is known as off-gassing and it is still not certain what harmful effects this might have. The safest option is to avoid potential health hazards and reduce the level of toxins found in your home by decorating with natural paints, fabrics and fibres.

Paints

Modern paint contains a soup of chemicals, ranging from heavy metals to volatile organic compounds (VOCs). These compounds turn into gas (that new paint smell) which in oil-based paint is given off for six months after application. Water-based paint contains less VOCs but has its own cocktail of toxic compounds that can off-gas for up to a year.

- **VOC content** – Choose paint with a low VOC content. Check the tin for information.

0% – 0.2%	minimal VOCs
0.3% – 7.99%	medium VOCs
8% – 50%	high VOCs
over 50%	very high VOCs

- **Organic or natural paint** – Preferably use these in order to bring the fewest toxins into your home.

Textiles

Textiles absorb sound and provide insulation but modern textiles, even those made with cotton, may have chemical residues which contain carcinogens and hormone disruptors and may cause headaches, dizziness, respiratory problems and difficulties with sleep, concentration and memory.

- **Natural textiles** – Textiles made with natural fibres are mostly produced with less processing and fewer chemicals. Vegetable-dyed wool, organic cotton, flax, linen, hemp and bamboo fabrics are good choices for bed linen and furnishings.

Floor covering

Carpets reduce draughts and noise but they are manufactured with noxious chemicals and harbour toxins, dust and pests.

- **Reduce off-gas toxins** – If appropriate, ask suppliers to leave new carpet unrolled for at least a week before fitting to allow more of the gases to be released.
- **Choose natural carpet** – Jute, sisal and coir are hardwearing and economic.
- **Linoleum** – Available in many colours, it is warm underfoot, made from long-lasting natural, biodegradable materials and suitable for areas subject to water splash.

• **Hard floor coverings** – Wood, slate and ceramic tiles, cork and bamboo are some of the healthiest options. Use wool or cotton rugs to maintain the comfort factor.

Furniture

Foil-wrapped or veneered self-assembly furniture is another source of chemical off-gases. Cheap to buy, it has a short useful life and then lies in a landfill site leaching toxins into the ground.

• **Solid wood furniture** – Invest in this instead of self-assembly panel furniture.

• **Repair, restore and re-work** – Old wooden furniture can be re-worked to keep it contemporary. Strip it back to a pale finish (using a water-based paint stripper or hot-air gun), or wax polish to its original glory. (See pages 20–21, *Green Cleaning*).

Air quality

For modern houses, the World Health Organisation recommends a complete change of air every two hours to avoid a build-up of toxins and maintain healthy oxygen levels. The most cost-effective way to do this is with air vents in walls and windows.

• **Detox** – In dry weather give your home a detox by opening windows for five minutes.

• **House plants** – They brighten up your home, help to maintain humidity and oxygen levels and absorb CO_2.

• **Fresher air** – Instead of using a commercial air freshener, add drops of essential oil to water in a mist sprayer or to a diffuser.

Did you know...?
The air inside most homes is actually more polluted than the air outside.

Right: Opening windows refreshes the air in your home.

RECYCLING

A lot of the things we throw away could be of use to someone else. With a little effort, unwanted items can be turned into cash or simply donated to a charity shop for fundraising, so it's worth considering other options before taking them to the dump or putting them out for rubbish collection and landfill.

How to recycle

Most local authorities provide boxes and bins for our recycling and collect them from outside our houses. This is a convenient and cost-effective way to recycle glass, cans newspaper and cardboard, clean clothes and fabric, garden waste and some plastic (check with your local authority). Be sure to separate your recycling waste to avoid contaminating the processes. Consider the following options for items which cannot be recycled in this way or may be of use to someone else.

- **Local newspaper** – An ad in the For Sale column of your local newspaper may be free or cost just a few pounds.
- **Car boot or garage sale** – A good option, especially in the summer months, to sell off all sorts of household and personal items.
- **Online auction sites** – A great way of selling almost anything.

- **Local charity shops** – Always glad to have clean clothes, books, bric-a-brac and in some areas, small items of furniture as well.

- **www.freecycle. org** – An online recycling network which works on a local basis. You post a message when you have something to give away or there is something that you need. Everything is free provided that the recipient collects. Keeping it local reduces transport costs to members and the environment.

What else can be recycled?

Most of what we buy is packaged, often several times over, and the contents of many homes are viewed as short term and disposable. The result is a huge and increasing amount of 'stuff' going into landfill sites. To find out if something can be recycled, and how, call the Waste and Resources Action Programme's (WRAP) Recycle Now helpline on 0845 331 3131.

Top: Kerbside collection has made recycling much easier for most people.

Below: If you don't have kerbside collection, sort your rubbish and take it to a recycling centre.

How and where to recycle

Aerosol cans
Seventy-five per cent of Local Authorities are now collecting empty aerosols through either kerbside schemes or recycling banks. Don't pierce or crush them.

Car batteries
Take to your local recycling centre.

CDs and DVDs
Take to charity shops. Try reusing computer disks as a bird scarer or as coasters – see *www.make-stuff.com* for more ideas.

Chemicals
Depends on the chemical. Contact local authority for advice.

Christmas trees
Some local authorities collect for shredding or you can get together with neighbours to hire a shredder and then compost. Avoid the problem by keeping a live tree in a big tub and stand it in the garden throughout the year.

Duvets and pillows
Wash man-made duvets and pillows, and donate to a charity shop. Natural fibres and feathers can be composted.

Electrical appliances
Take to your local recycling centre. Several charities recycle computers (see *www.computeraid.org*). See *www.mercuryrecycling.co.uk* for TV screens and monitors.

Engine oil
Take to your local recycling centre. Never burn or pour it down the drain.

Fluorescent light bulbs
Can be taken to some recycling centres. (Alternatively see *www.mercuryrecycling.co.uk*).

Fridges and freezers
Old models contain CFCs but recycling centres will accept them for specialist recycling. Or you can arrange with your local council for removal, usually for a fee.

Medical products
Take all unused medicines to a pharmacy or doctor's surgery. Take hearing aids to Age Concern charity shops, hospital audio department or GP's surgery. (See *www.reuze.co.uk*).

Mobile phones
Most mobile phone retailers will recycle old phones. Some supermarkets will also take them and make a donation to charity. *www.envirofone.com* will give you money for them.

Packaging
Polythene is recyclable; see *www.recoup.org* for which other plastics can be recycled. Some recycling centres will take bubble wrap (see *www.recyclenow.com*).

Paint
See *www.communityrepaint.org.uk* for re-use. Go to local recycling centre for safe disposal.

Printer cartridges
Several charities will reuse or recycle cartridges (see *www.recyclingappeal.com*). Make use of the recycling bins found in computer or charity shops, or use freepost return envelopes.

Water filters
Send six at a time to Brita Recycling, FREEPOST NAT 17876, Bicester, OX26 4BR or look out for a collection point in stores such as Argos and Robert Dyas.

For more information on how and where to recycle, see Useful Websites, page 95.

IN THE GARDEN

Going green and taking an organic approach to gardening saves money from the word go. Many of the changes are easy to make — watering with harvested water instead of a sprinkler attached to the mains water supply; encouraging wildlife and natural predators; not buying chemical pesticides and fertilisers or commercial composts and mulches. The savings soon mount up and if you grow your own vegetables and flowers for cutting, the rewards are even greater. It may take a season or two and a bit of adjustment before the garden finds its natural balance, but a little patience and the more relaxed approach results in a low maintenance garden with a positive impact on the environment, more beneficial insects and visiting birds, fewer slugs and pests and much healthier plants.

Left: Use home-made compost on raised beds to reuse waste and keep the soil healthy.

THE BALANCED GARDEN

The balanced garden is all about working with nature, not against it. By not using synthetic garden aids, such as chemical pesticides and fertilisers, and by taking advantage of natural and available resources, your garden can be low maintenance, sustainable and productive.

Green garden design

A green garden doesn't have to be all vegetation and no space for relaxation.

- **Patios and decking** – Help to make your garden an extension of your living space. Timber for decking should be from a sustainable source (see *www.tda.org.uk).*
- **Reclamation yards** – Good for getting old bricks, paving and garden features.
- **Rainwater** – Consider installing rainwater storage under a new patio or lawn.
- **Solar lighting** – Can be used around the garden to reduce energy consumption.
- **Hardy plants** – Grow plants that are drought-resistant and hardy.

Groundwork

This is when the long-term structure of the garden is laid. It saves expense if you plan and consider environmental implications.

- **Vegetable patch** – These require a level area with plenty of light.
- **Raised beds** – These increase the planting area. Once dug they can be annually topped up with compost – the worms will keep the soil healthy and aerated and the beds won't need to be dug over again.

Front gardens

Front gardens are environmentally important not only as a green space but as a soakaway for rainfall. Instead of laying tarmac or paving, plant into gravel or chippings – it's low maintenance and much greener.

- **Surfaces** – At about £30 a tonne delivered, 14mm clean stone is a much cheaper alternative to pea-gravel or slate. Choose permeable (porous) material for driveways.
- **Approval** – Most garden landscaping doesn't require any planning permission. Covering an area of your front garden that is more than 5sq m (5.8sq yd) with non-porous material is the exception. Average cost of the application is £200.
- **Renewable energy** – If you're planning some major landscaping, consider installing a ground source heat pump, for potential energy savings of over 50 per cent (See pages 10–11, *Energy Efficiency).*

Right: A balanced garden should work with nature; butterflies and bees are a sign you're getting it right.

Outdoor living

Garden centres offer a huge range of products for outdoor living, but many of these are manufactured from plastics or non-sustainable woods and shipped around the world.

£ Choose a chimenea
A terracotta or iron chimenea costs from £50 and burning waste wood is free and releases no more carbon dioxide than if it was decayed.

- **Heaters** – The amount of CO_2 generated by patio heaters is cancelling out other emission-saving initiatives. The heat from one 12.5kW gas cylinder produces around 35kg of CO_2 in the 13 hours before it runs out of gas. Use a chimenea (a freestanding oven) instead and burn carbon-neutral waste and garden wood or British-made charcoal. Greenest of all, put on a jumper.

- **Barbecues** – Gas barbecues aren't used for as long as gas heaters but still emit carbon dioxide. Use a charcoal barbecue and cook your food on charcoal obtained from a sustainable source.

- **Sustainable sources** – Only buy garden furniture with the Forest Stewardship Council (FSC) label.

Rainwater/greywater

On hot summer days, over 70 per cent of the domestic water supply may be used for watering gardens. Installing water diverters and storage can supply enough recycled water to keep your garden in peak condition and reduce your water bill.

- **Rainwater butts** – Connect to the guttering down pipes and attach a hosepipe with a trigger control. Your watering will be easier and much more efficient. Save money by buying a discounted water butt – available from the various regional water suppliers.

- **Bath and shower water** – Fit a permanent diverter to your bathroom plumbing and reuse bath and shower water on the garden – any soap in the water will discourage aphids. A less permanent solution is to draw off the bathwater using a hosepipe with a suction control.

Encouraging wildlife

Resident wildlife is essential for the balance of any garden, large or small. It can help to keep pest populations under control without the use of chemicals.

- **Dig a pond** – Even a small pond under 1m (3ft 3in) across is enough to attract frogs, newts and toads. Make sure there is a slope for access and enough damp nooks and crannies nearby for shelter and they will reward the effort by keeping the slug population in check.

- **Go wild** – Leave a small area of the garden uncultivated or sow grasses and wild flowers. The undergrowth will attract wildlife including hedgehogs (which eat slugs), insects and butterflies.

- **Leave nettles** – Nettles attract butterflies and provide the basis for an excellent liquid plant feed (see pages 36–37, *Plant and Lawn Care*).

- **Slow-worms** – Your compost bin is the perfect habitat for slow-worms, toads and hedgehogs which all eat slugs – just keep an eye out for them when turning or emptying the bin.

Above: Hedgehogs will keep pests such as slugs under control.

- **Encourage bees** – Bees are necessary for pollination, so grow bee-friendly plants such as laurel (one of the earliest providers of nectar), wallflowers and borage, lupins, geraniums, hollyhocks and lavender.
- **Bat boxes** – Put bat boxes up to encourage bats, which eat gnats and mosquitoes by the thousand.

Natural predators

Pesticides have become an easy convenience but, as well as presenting a health hazard, they undermine the healthy balance of the garden. In addition to small mammals such as hedgehogs and slow worms, there are a variety of nematodes (microscopic organisms) which can be used to control a range of pests, especially greenhouse pests such as red spider mite.

- **Not all bad** – Slugs have a valuable part to play in composting all the vegetation and garden waste that doesn't make it to the compost heap. Unlike pesticides, natural predators will maintain a healthy balance of the slug population.
- **Predatory nematodes** – Can be used instead of chemical sprays to control garden pests biologically. Available from garden centres, the nematodes are added to water and sprayed onto the garden or in the greenhouse in spring.

Carbon-neutral gardening

Many gardening tasks and activities can be carbon-neutral and reduce domestic greenhouse gases. However, carbon from fossil fuels is consumed in petrol and electricity-powered garden equipment, heated greenhouses, floodlighting, patio heating and a host of other equipment.

- **Heated greenhouses** – These are one of the biggest consumers of energy in the garden. Bring tender plants into the house (they will improve the air quality) and if you must have a greenhouse, insulate it with bubble wrap in winter.
- **Choose wood** – Don't use gas or electrically powered heaters and barbecues – burning wood does release carbon but no more than if it was left to decompose.
- **Lawnmowers** – If your lawn isn't very big, get fit with a manual lawnmower.
- **Plant trees** – They absorb carbon dioxide and pollution, and give off oxygen. Apple or plum trees are great if you want to make your own desserts or jam.

Did you know...?
The total area of paved front gardens in London is equivalent to the area of 5,200 football pitches.
Source: The London Assembly

GROWING YOUR OWN

Home-grown vegetables, herbs and fruit, freshly picked and packed with flavour and nutrients, has to be the best way to enjoy your recommended five-a-day. Growing your own isn't difficult, it saves you money and you don't even need a large garden or dedicated vegetable patch to do it.

Getting started

Growing your own plants from seed is the best way to establish your vegetable growing but if this isn't possible, local nurseries and plant sales are a good source of locally grown plants. Raising plants doesn't have to be wholesale – a tomato plant or two and a courgette plant is enough for a small family.

- **The essentials** – The key to successfully growing your own is sunlight, good soil, sufficient watering and good drainage.
- **Seeds** – If you have the time and space, grow from seeds. Exchange seeds and seedlings with other growers to save money and get a wider variety of produce.
- **Pricey produce** – Where space is limited, grow produce that is expensive to buy (asparagus, raspberries, strawberries). They take a season to establish but will crop for several years.

- **Gardening clubs** – Join your local gardening club. Membership fees vary but with access to local gardening know-how and the possibility of loaning those expensive and not-often-needed tools, you will gain more than just recovering the fee.

Mixed borders

Lots of vegetables will grow just as happily among your flowers as long as they have enough light and space. So you don't need a dedicated vegetable patch. They can also have a mutually beneficial effect and help to maintain a healthy balance in the garden, avoiding any need for chemicals.

- **Onions** – Grow onions around your roses to help to keep green and blackfly away.
- **Tagetes** – These pungent French marigolds are confusing to a range of flies that would otherwise be intent on your vegetables. They are particularly useful around carrots.

£ Your own herbs

Grow a selection of herbs in a sunny spot, in the ground or in a container, and save yourself money at the supermarket.

Containers

Don't be put off because your outdoor space is a courtyard or a balcony, you can still grow your own in a variety of containers.

- **Reuse** – Containers don't have to be expensive: recycle old buckets, washing-up bowls, washed out 5 litre (1 gall) paint tins. Anything more than 30cm (12in) wide and 45cm (18in) deep can grow herbs, vegetables and fruits such as strawberries and blueberries. Make drainage holes and keep the containers regularly watered.
- **Potatoes** – Plastic tubs are perfect for growing potatoes, especially the salad varieties that are so expensive to buy. Just three to five sprouting potatoes will produce 2.5–3kg (5–6lb) of new potatoes.
- **Windowsills** – A well-secured window box, preferably more than 30cm (12in) deep, on a sunny sill is enough space to grow shallow-rooted herbs, salad leaves, dwarf French beans and peas.

Vegetable patch and allotments

The ultimate in growing your own is to have a dedicated vegetable patch in your garden or to rent an allotment.

- **Vegetable gardens** – These can have as much interest as a flowerbed. Grow nasturtiums and violas for additional colour and you can eat the flowers too.
- **Allotments** – The average allotment plot, 9m x 6m (30ft x 20ft), can make a significant reduction to your food budget. The average national cost is £25 a year though there are waiting lists in some areas. (For information and to find your nearest allotment, see *www.nsalg.org.uk*).

> ### Did you know...?
> In warmer areas of the UK, even peppers, chillies and aubergines can grow successfully in containers in sheltered spots.

Above: Parsnips are easy to grow and, once they've germinated, need very little maintenance.

EASY COMPOSTING

Making your own compost is a great money saver and beneficial to the environment too. Some local authorities will collect garden waste for composting but make your own and you'll reduce all the CO_2 emissions associated with disposing of your garden waste and then buying commercial compost. Making compost is free, convenient and just about as eco-friendly as you can get.

The compost bin

A heap in the corner of your garden will work just as well but it's not very pretty and it's easier if the materials are contained in some way. Compost bins come in all shapes and sizes and most local authorities have a discount scheme for householders to buy a basic one.

- **Make it yourself** – Save up to £50 with a homemade compost bin. Reuse old bricks, pallets and wooden crates.
- **Use tyres** – Old tyres make a very versatile system that doesn't take up too much space. Stack them on top of each other (the weight will hold them in place) and cover the top (an old bucket lid will usually do the job). As the contents break down,

lift the top tyres off to start a new stack.
- **Old dustbins** – If a wheelie bin has made your dustbin redundant, cut away the bottom and then use it in exactly the same way as a purpose-made compost bin.

What can be composted?

Compost needs a good balance of nitrogen-rich material (kitchen and garden waste) with carbon-rich material (hedge and woody trimmings and scrunched up paper or cardboard). The ratio of nitrogen-rich to carbon-rich materials should be 50:50.

> **£ Don't buy, make!**
> Making compost is free and it saves you buying compost, mulching material and commercial soil conditioners.

- **A simple rule** – If it used to be growing, it can be composted.
- **Start with the wood** – Start the heap with woody material to allow airflow.
- **Small layers** – Never add more than a 15cm (6in) layer of any single type of material – it will turn the heap into a soggy mess that doesn't smell too good.

Wormeries

A really productive solution for kitchen peelings is a wormery, especially if you don't have space for a compost heap. Usually supplied complete with worms, commercial wormeries are a stack of trays on a stand, with a tap at the base. Kitchen peelings are placed in the top tray, and within a few weeks the worms convert the peelings into a lovely rich compost.

- **Temperature** – Wormeries are a living habitat that doesn't function below 10°C (50°F) or above 30°C (86°F) so be sure to keep it frost-free in the winter and out of direct sunlight in summer. The ideal temperature for a wormery is between 15°C (59°F) and 20°C (68°F).
- **Plant feed** – The liquid that drains to the bottom tray makes a really good plant feed. Dilute 1:10 parts rainwater. See pages 36–37, *Plant and Lawn Care*.

Did you know...?

At least 40 per cent of household waste can be composted and used in the garden.

Source: Waste and Resources Action Programme (WRAP)

DON'T BIN IT!

All the following can be composted:
Paper-based materials (e.g. scrunched-up cardboard)
Fabric made from natural fibres (e.g. torn-up clothing made from cotton, silk, linen, wool) – don't be impatient with these, they will take a very long time to compost
Used teabags and coffee grounds
Eggshells
Wood ash

BIN IT!

The following cannot be composted:
Cooked foods, oils and fats (They will compost but they might also attract rats.)
Nappies and the faeces from cat litter trays
Whole newspapers, telephone directories, glossy printed paper and laminated cardboard packaging
Diseased plants and perennial weeds (Bindweed and dandelions will love your compost heap. These are the exception for municipal waste or a bonfire!)

PLANT AND LAWN CARE

Maintaining the garden with a green approach is cost effective and very satisfying. It means avoiding quick-fixes so no chemical products or high maintenance watering – but the long-term result is a much healthier garden that can cope with the vagaries of the weather and a little neglect when necessary. It will also support garden wildlife.

Maintaining the lawn

For many gardeners keeping the lawn fresh and green is hard work and expensive, involving a great deal of time feeding, mowing, raking and irrigating with vast amounts of water. But the average lawn is a remarkably hardy mix of grasses that will survive the driest summer – even when it goes brown, the next fall of rain will soon perk it up again.

- **Mowing** – Mow the lawn with blades at a higher setting and leave the clippings where they fall. Within a few days they will have worked down and around the roots, keeping them cool and moist.
- **Watering** – Even in hot dry weather the lawn only needs a thorough watering once a week, preferably in the evening.

Mulching and feeding

Healthy soil is the basis of green gardening. Good soil that is not too free-draining will ensure that essential nutrients aren't washed away when it rains. Some plants benefit from plant feeds which can be made very easily.

- **Mulching** – Improve the soil structure by mulching the flower and vegetable beds with compost or farm manure. The worms will soon take it down below the surface. Use grass cuttings to mulch around plants and conserve moisture.
- **Plant feeds** – Commercial fertilisers and plant feeds are expensive. Save money by making your own plant feed using wormery drain-off or crushed or chopped nettles soaked in a bucket of water for a few weeks. In both cases, dilute the liquid 1:10 (to about the colour of tea for the nettles) and apply with a watering can. If you go for the nettle option, keep adding nettles to the bucket until winter for a continuing supply, then put the remaining sludge onto the compost heap.

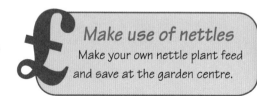

Make use of nettles
Make your own nettle plant feed and save at the garden centre.

Watering the garden

Watering the garden is often regarded as a summertime necessity but much of our garden watering doesn't reach the plant roots and simply evaporates or runs-off.

- **Plastic bottles** – Re-use plastic bottles by cutting off the base and pushing the bottle, upside down into the ground next to thirsty plants. It directs water to the roots.
- **Avoid evaporation** – In hot weather a good drenching every few days is more effective than frequent surface watering. Water the base of plants not the foliage.

Weed control

Weeds compete with your plants for moisture and nutrients. It's easy to spray them off with weed killer or torch them with a garden weed gun, but these solutions damage the garden. There are greener ways to get rid of them without chemicals.

- **Hoeing** – Get in the habit of hoeing the flowerbed – a quick job that culls weeds before they've got going.
- **Suppress weeds** – Applying a good layer of mulching material will do the job.

Caring for container plants

Garden tubs and containers are a useful way to extend the growing area but they do need regular watering – place them in a saucer to help to conserve water.

Above: Help target your watering using a cut-off plastic bottle.

ECO-TRAVEL

We take covering long distances in very short times for granted, often work miles from our homes and take our well-earned holidays in distant corners of the world. But travel is by its nature a polluting activity and is responsible for a quarter of the UK's CO_2 emissions. It has been estimated that by 2050, the environmental cost of flying will exceed the UK's entire emissions budget. Fortunately, there are many things you can do to reduce the impact of your travel, and even bring benefits to the places you are visiting. What is more, most of them will save you money.

Left: Taking the train rather than driving or flying is one of the most effective ways of cutting your carbon footprint.

GREENER TRAVEL

The average Briton travels 7,000 miles a year inside the UK – and 80 per cent of those journeys are made by car. Few of us can stop driving altogether, but just reducing the number of car journeys you make is a simple way to cut your carbon footprint. With the high cost of petrol, this will cut your costs at the same time.

Active choices

A quarter of all car journeys are two miles or less so many of these trips could be done on foot. For longer distances, consider cycling – once you've bought your bike, there are minimal running costs and no parking fees.

- **Avoid short car trips** – Mile for mile, these are more polluting than long ones – the

engine uses more fuel while it is warming up, and the catalytic converter in the exhaust is less efficient when it is cold.

- **Walk** – It's good for you and totally free.
- **Get on your bike** – Three-quarters of us live within two miles of a signed cycle route – find out where your nearest one is on the website of sustainable transport charity Sustrans (*www.sustrans.org*). Some councils offer subsidised urban cycle training; ask your local authority for details.

Public transport

Buses and other forms of public transport are far more energy-efficient per passenger than cars, so use them when you can.

- **No excuses** – Nearly 90 per cent of us live within walking distance of a bus stop.
- **Get informed** – Find the quickest way to get to your destination by public transport with the Department for Transport's door-to-door journey planner (*www. transportdirect.info*). It also calculates the amount of CO_2 produced by your journey.

Cutting back on the car

If you naturally reach for the car keys every time you go out, start to break the habit by having one car-free day a week. Also, take

£ *Cheaper train travel*
Taking the train can be more expensive than driving, especially for more than one passenger. Reduce your fares by travelling off-peak, booking in advance, and using a railcard. Websites such as *www.nationalrail.co.uk* are worth checking for special offers.

some time to think about other ways you can cut down on car usage.

- **Double up on errands** – Make maximum use of your car to cut down on the number of trips you make. For example, if you drive to see a friend, do the shopping on the way home. You'll save on fuel and time.

- **Go online** – Buying on the internet saves you from driving to a store. Use this for regular groceries and other purchases that you don't need to see before you buy. Some supermarkets offer green delivery slots so your purchases are delivered at the same time as someone else in your area.

- **Share the school run** – Almost a fifth of the cars on the UK's urban roads during morning rush hour are carrying children to the school gates. Pooling resources with another family means you only need to drive on alternate days – halving both your emissions and costs. It's worth checking whether your children's school has a travel plan, such as a 'walking bus' or 'cycle train' in which children travel to school on foot or by bike in supervised groups.

- **Lift-share** – If you make other regular journeys, see if you can travel with a neighbour or acquaintance in return for a contribution to petrol costs. Websites such as *www.liftshare.com* may be able to put you in touch with someone willing to share your journey if you have a regular commute. (See also *Business Travel*, pages 90–91.)

Above: Cycling in congested cities can often get you where you are going more quickly than taking the car.

CHOOSING A GREENER CAR

Cars are one exception to the green rule that old is better than new. Modern cars are generally more fuel efficient and produce fewer emissions than older vehicles. Catalytic converters, which convert exhaust pollutants into harmless products, have made cars cleaner: a pre-1992 car with no catalytic converter can be 20 times more polluting than a new car.

Fuel efficiency

Look for a car with a fuel-efficient engine; it will be cheaper to run and a lot better for the environment.

- **Efficiency ratings** – Like fridges and washing machines, new cars now receive an efficiency rating ranging from A (for the most fuel-efficient models) to G (the most polluting). The information should be available at the showroom.
- **Vehicle Certification Agency** – Has its own database of cars listing fuel efficiency, estimated fuel costs and environmental impact (see *www.vcacarfueldata.org.uk*).
- **Society of Motor Manufacturers and Traders** – Its database has CO_2 emissions for all cars registered since 1997 – useful if you are buying secondhand (see *www.*

smmt.co.uk). However, in general you should avoid driving very old cars as they are significantly more polluting.

- **Automatic or manual?** – Automatic cars use about 10 per cent more fuel than manuals, while cars with continuously variable transmission (CVT) use about five per cent more. Consider a car with automated manual transmission; in which, electronic and hydraulic systems manage the clutch and gear change without significantly increasing fuel consumption.

£ Save with a green car
If you are buying a small family car, opting for a fuel-efficient model could shave almost 30 per cent off your fuel bill.* Greener cars not only save you money on fuel bills; they are also liable for less road tax.
Source: Friends of the Earth

Types of fuel

The best choice of fuel for you will depend on the sort of driving that you do.

- **Diesel** – Do not assume that diesel cars are necessarily the greener choice. Although they use less fuel than petrol cars, they produce more nitrogen oxides, particulates and other toxic emissions. Generally speaking, a diesel car is a better option if you do a lot of motorway driving. But if you live in an urban area, where air quality is more of a concern, go for petrol-driven cars.

- **Electric cars** – Worth considering if you only use a car for short trips. They can be charged from an ordinary socket, and costs work out around one pence a mile. Exemption from road tax, parking fees and congestion charges in some cities make them very cheap to run with one manufacturer claiming that you can recoup the cost of the car within a year. An electric scooter is another green option that you might want to consider if you do not need to carry passengers.
- **Hybrid cars** – These combine an electric motor and battery with a petrol engine; the electric motor charges as you drive and then powers the car at lower speeds. They are pricier than standard cars to buy, but running costs are lower. Hybrids are ideal for town driving as the start/stop work uses the regenerative brakes which recharge the batteries. If you do a lot of motorway driving, the benefits are less obvious.

Which wheels?

Buy the smallest car that suits your everyday needs. If you need a larger car once or twice a year, it may be cheaper to buy a smaller car and rent the larger one when you need it.

- **Four-wheel drives** – Burn between four and 14 per cent more fuel than a standard vehicle with the same load-carrying capacity. As well as costing you more in fuel, they also incur higher vehicle excise duties and, in some areas, higher parking permit fees as well.
- **Car clubs** – Give you access to a new, fuel-efficient car for an annual fee – you book and pay for your slots through a website. If you need a car only occasionally, this is a significantly cheaper option than maintaining and insuring your own vehicle. See *www.carclubs.org.uk* for details of your nearest club.

Above: Don't assume that diesel is the greener option. It depends on your car usage.

DRIVING GREENER

When it comes to reducing the environmental impact of your driving, it is not just what you drive that counts but also the way that you drive it. The basic principle is this: the harder your engine has to work, the more fuel it has to burn, and the more CO_2 emissions are produced. So, if you go easy on your engine, you automatically use less fuel – saving you money and cutting the cost of your driving to the planet.

Taking care of your car

A poorly maintained car is likely to use more fuel and pump out more pollution. It won't last as long either.

- **Regular servicing** – Keeps your car in good working order.
- **Tyre pressure** – Soft tyres increase rolling resistance, making the engine use more fuel. Check your tyre pressure regularly, and before every long journey. Refer to your car manual for the correct tyre pressure, remembering that it may vary depending on the load. This will extend the life of your tyres, saving you money too.
- **Engine oil** – Using the recommended grade of engine oil can improve your fuel efficiency by one to two per cent.

Before you go

A little planning before you set off can help to reduce your fuel consumption.

- **Reduce load** – A heavy car uses more fuel, so don't carry anything that you don't need. Clear the boot and take off bike racks or roof boxes when not in use.
- **Plan your route** – Getting lost makes you drive further and use more fuel. If you are going somewhere unfamiliar, take a few minutes to plan your journey before you leave. The AA website (*www.theAA.com*) has a comprehensive route planner as well as up-to-date regional traffic news.
- **Avoid congestion** – If you can choose when to drive, steer clear of busy times. You'll use less fuel on a clear run than if you have to keep stopping and starting.

On the road

Simple measures once you are on the road can also make a difference.

- **Don't dawdle** – Start your engine when you're ready to go and leave promptly. If you're likely to be stationary for more than three minutes, turn off the engine.
- **Think ahead** – Accelerate gently, and keep a close eye on the road ahead to avoid unnecessary braking. When you have to

Right: Checking your tyre pressure regularly makes your tyres last longer and reduces your fuel consumption.

£

Cut fuel costs

Following eco-driving tips could reduce the average driver's fuel costs by eight per cent* – around £140 a year.

Source: Department for Transport

slow down or stop, release the accelerator in plenty of time, keeping your car in gear.

- **Avoid labouring the engine** – This makes it work harder, and burn more fuel, as well as putting extra strain on components such as the oil pump. Reducing revs can have a significant effect on fuel consumption. Try changing gear when the revs are around 2000rpm in a diesel car, or 2500rpm in a petrol car. Some new cars now feature gear shift indicators, which inform the driver of the optimum time to change gear.

- **Slow down** – You use less petrol if you drive more slowly. When you are doing 70mph you could be using around nine per cent more fuel than at 60mph and 15 per cent more than at 50mph.

- **Cut down on air con** – Don't leave the air con on all the time. If you are driving slowly around town, opening the windows is a greener way to cool down. But on the motorway, having the windows open increases drag so put on your air con for a few minutes, then switch to the blowers.

- **Electrical gadgets** – Using the heated rear windows or headlights increases your fuel consumption, so turn them off when you don't need them.

THE FLYING ISSUE

Air travel is the fastest-growing contributor to global warming and Britons are keener on flying than any other European nation, with almost half of us flying at least once a year.

Low-fly zone

Flying less is the quickest way to reduce your carbon footprint. Calculations of CO_2 emissions from flying vary widely, but a return flight to New York could release around 1.3 tonnes of CO_2 per passenger.

- **Take a no-fly pledge** – See *www.lowflyzone.org* to strengthen your resolve.
- **Cut down on flying** – If you can't give up flying altogether, set yourself an annual

Did you know...?

Air travel accounts for 3.5 per cent of greenhouse gas emissions worldwide*, and 7 per cent in the UK. The figures may seem low, but the negative effects of vapour trails and exhaust emissions released high in the atmosphere mean that the damage may be much worse than the statistics suggest.

Source: Intergovernmental Panel on Climate Change (IPCC)

target of, say, one return flight a year, to help you to reduce the amount you fly.

- **Go short-haul** – If what you want from your holiday is to lie on a beach, head for a European destination rather than the Seychelles. Short-haul flights emit more CO_2 per mile, but have less impact on the environment than long-hauls because they use less fuel overall – and they're cheaper.
- **Fly less, stay longer** – One long trip will have a lower environmental impact than two short ones. Spending more time in a country also gives you an opportunity to explore areas off the tourist route, ensuring that your money benefits local communities (see *Be an Eco-Tourist*, pages 48–49).
- **Stay in the UK** – It gives you a chance to explore your own country and can be a lot cheaper than going abroad.
- **Go by train** – It's greener than flying, and almost as quick once you factor in the time at the airport. Three-quarters of flights in 2006 were to European destinations, many of which could be reached by train. See *www.seat61.com* for details of how to get almost anywhere by train and boat.
- **Go by sea** – Take slower freight or car ferries – high-speed passenger ferries can emit as much CO_2 as planes.

Right: When the weather is on your side, a UK beach holiday can be as relaxing as one on foreign shores.

... and if you fly

If you must fly, there are still ways to limit the environmental impact.

- **Leave the car at home** – Most airports have good public transport links so use these to reduce air pollution in the surrounding area and save on parking fees.
- **Travel light** – The reason your luggage is weighed at check-in is so that the airline can calculate the amount of fuel needed for the journey. If everyone packs less, then the aeroplane's fuel consumption is lower.
- **Go paperfree** – Electronic tickets are one small step towards greener flying.
- **Take a packed lunch** – This avoids expensive and highly packaged food at airports and on aeroplanes.

- **Carbon offsetting** – This involves paying a company to carry out an activity to reduce the amount of CO_2 in the atmosphere by the same amount as your journey has generated. Schemes vary widely in effectiveness, so choose yours carefully. The Voluntary Carbon Standard (VCS) (*www.v-c-s.org*) may be able to help, while Carbon Balanced (*www.carbonbalanced.org*) is run by the UK-based charity World Land Trust.

£ **Hidden costs**
Airports, unlike railway stations, tend to be out of town so factor in transfer to accommodation when comparing costs.

BE AN ECO-TOURIST

There's no doubt that our holidays have an environmental impact but on the other hand, tourism is a major source of revenue for some of the world's poorest countries. Thinking carefully about where you stay can help to reduce the environmental negatives of your travel, and is a good way of ensuring that your trip has a positive impact on the local economy.

Low-carbon accommodation

Hotels are often not the greenest, or the cheapest, accommodation option.

- **Do it yourself** – Self-catering allows you to control energy and water use, and to guard against food waste, more easily than when you are staying in a hotel.
- **Get back to nature** – Camping is the greenest holiday. If done responsibly, it does very little environmental damage.
- **Swap your home** – Register with a house-swapping organisation – you pay a small annual membership fee but save on your accommodation costs. Insurers generally do not charge extra for this, but keep them informed.
- **Homestays** – Some tour operators offer the option of staying with a local family.

It's often inexpensive, and a great way of getting an insight into their way of life. Make sure the family receives a substantial proportion of the money you pay.

- **Go local** – If you must stay in a hotel, choose a locally owned one or an independent guest house rather than a chain hotel to help to keep your money in the community that you are visiting.
- **Avoid all-inclusive resorts** – You will be buying your accommodation, food and day trips from one company that is usually based outside the country you are visiting.
- **Save energy** – Make your hotel stay greener by unplugging appliances that you don't need. Switch off the air conditioning when you leave the room or avoid using it altogether. Opt out of daily room service and ask for clean towels and linen only when you need them. Use your own soap rather than the free toiletries; they use a lot of packaging for relatively little product.

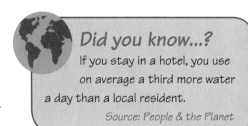

Did you know...?
If you stay in a hotel, you use on average a third more water a day than a local resident.
Source: People & the Planet

Eco-tourism

Eco-tourism is a buzzword, but there's no clear agreement on what it means. Don't assume a self-styled eco-resort or hotel is green; check its policies on energy and water consumption and waste management.

- **Association of Independent Tour Operators (AITO)** – Its members must adhere to sustainable tourism guidelines. (See *www.aito.co.uk*).
- **The International Ecotourism Society** – Promotes eco-tourism and responsible travel. (See *www.ecotourism.org*).

On holiday

You don't need to spend your holiday worrying about being green, just take a few simple measures to limit the environmental impact of your trip – and save you money.

- **Think waste** – Remove packaging from your toiletries before you leave so that you can be sure they are recycled. Choose environmentally friendly products to minimise your contribution to the pollution of water supplies. Bring home potentially toxic waste such as used batteries.
- **Protect wildlife** – When visiting wildlife parks or World Heritage sites, don't stray outside the designated areas. Shun anything that is made from endangered animals or plants (such as ivory souvenirs).
- **Don't hire a car** – Use public transport – or better still walk or cycle. You'll see more, and it's cheaper and less stressful.
- **Eat like a local** – Look out for local brands of food or drink rather than imported ones. They will almost certainly be cheaper and doing this is an easy way of ensuring that your money gets into the local economy.

Above: Responsible camping does very little environmental damage and really lets you get away from it all.

ECO-SHOPPING

In our consumer culture, shopping has become something we do for fun – there's nothing wrong with that but one consequence is that almost all of us end up with things we do not really need or want. Our urge to spend money is a drain on our personal finances, and on the world's resources. Greener shopping doesn't have to mean adopting an austere way of life, or even enjoying ourselves any less. It simply means buying what you need, when you need it.

Thinking about where your shopping comes from is the next step. Whether it is looking for an organic label, buying from a company that respects the environment, or buying second-hand – it's all part of going green.

Left: Food at a farmers' market is fresh, tasty and generally uses very little packaging.

CUT YOUR FOOD WASTE

You can save yourself hundreds of pounds a year – and reduce your waste – just by changing the way that you shop. Britons throw away roughly a third of everything they buy, and more than half that food is edible at the moment it is binned. As a nation we chuck out 5,500 whole chickens, 1.3 million yoghurts, and 440,000 ready meals every day.

How to shop

Before you do a big shop, plan your meals for the next few days. Check your fridge and cupboards to avoid unnecessary purchases. Think about leftovers when planning your meals, too. If you're having a Sunday roast, plan to cook chicken risotto or curry the next day, and use the carcass for stock for soup.

- **Have a 'basics cupboard'** – Allows you to supplement leftovers and cook simple meals without resorting to pricey, highly packaged takeaways. As you finish things, add them to an ongoing shopping list.
- **Store food correctly** – Keeping food in the right way helps to avoid unnecessary waste. See *www.eatwell.gov.uk* for general information on storing food, and *www.lovefoodhatewaste.com* for tips on keeping food fresh for longer.
- **Shop with a list** – Be sure to stick to it as impulse buys often end up in the bin.
- **Ignore supermarket promotions** – Special offers are designed to encourage you to buy more, not to spend less, so avoid them unless they are things that you planned to buy or are certain you will use.
- **Buy perishables little and often** – If you buy fruit once a week in bulk, you are likely to chuck some of it out. If you throw away half the bananas you buy, each banana you eat effectively costs you twice the price.

£ *Bin less to save more*
Planning your meals better and eliminating unnecessary wastage of food could save your household around £420 a year – £610 if you have children.
Source: Waste and Resources Action Programme (WRAP)

What to cook

Being organised about your cooking can dramatically cut waste and save you money.

Above right: Measure out portions carefully to reduce waste – and your waistline!

Right: Making a list will help you to avoid impulse buys which often end up in the bin.

- **Check the date** – Make a mental note of use-by dates on perishables. The best-before date refers to quality rather than safety, so (with the important exception of eggs) food can be eaten after this date as long as it has been stored correctly. Eat it as soon as you can (and before the use-by date) for best flavour and texture.
- **Freeze it** – Put freezable food in the freezer if you're not sure when you'll eat it.
- **Get clever with leftovers** – Freeze leftovers as a quick meal; pour the dregs of a bottle of wine into ice-cube trays and freeze to add to sauces or gravy; use overripe fruit in delicious smoothies.
- **Portion control** – When it comes to cereals, it is easy to cook too much and end up throwing the extra away. Instead of

guesstimating how much rice or pasta to cook, measure it. A teacup of rice is plenty for two adults. One bowl of dried pasta equals about two bowls of cooked pasta.

Did you know...?

Eliminating food waste could cut CO_2 emissions by 18 million tonnes – equivalent to taking one in five cars off the road.

Source: Waste and Resources Action Programme (WRAP)

EATING GREEN

It is sometimes hard to know what constitutes the green food option. Is it better to buy locally produced apples or should you plump for imported organic ones? One thing is certain: it pays to know where your food comes from and how it is produced. Though ethically sourced food sometimes carries a higher price tag, there are ways to reduce the cost.

Reducing packaging

Highly packaged items come at a cost – it has been estimated that the average British household spends a sixth of its total food budget on packaging. Try these tips to cut down on packaging.

- **Think recycling** – Choose goods that come in containers you can recycle locally – glass, tin, etc. Avoid hard-to-recycle packaging such as polystyrene. If possible, compost paper and cardboard.
- **Buy direct** – Organic fruit and vegetables from the supermarket are often heavily packaged so buy from a farmers' market or sign up to an organic box scheme. See *www.farmersmarkets.net* for details of farmers' markets and *www.boxscheme.org* for listings of box schemes.

- **Ban the bag** – The average person gets through 134 plastic carrier bags a year, most of which are simply thrown away. Keep a few bags in the boot of the car, by the front door, or in your bike panniers so that you have them to hand when you need them. An increasing number of retailers are now charging for bags, so this green measure will save you money, too.
- **Go refillable** – Some healthfood stores sell refillable cleaning products, such as washing-up liquid and bathroom cleaner. It works out cheaper than buying a new bottle each time and saves on packaging.
- **Buy produce loose** – Look for stores that sell small food items such as nuts and dried fruit from large containers; you can transfer them to paper bags, avoiding the need for plastic packaging.
- **Get basics in bulk** – Rice, for example, can cost half the price if you buy a small sack rather than a kilo or two. Split your purchases with a friend or neighbour if you don't have enough storage space.

Sound food

Thinking about what we buy can save us money, reduce the environmental impact and improve the flavour of our cooking.

- **Follow the seasons** – Buying food in seaon is a good way to reduce energy used to produce it, therefore reducing greenhouse gas emissions. Fruit and vegetables that are in season are usually cheaper to buy and taste better too.
- **Go local** – Choose produce from local suppliers to reduce the distance your food has to travel. Supermarkets have to favour varieties that travel or refrigerate well (for example, most supermarket strawberries are Elsanta, which has a long shelf life). So you may find that your fruit and vegetables taste better – and are fresher – if you buy local.
- **Think organic** – Organic fruit and vegetables (look for the Soil Association label) are produced in a more sustainable

> ### Did you know...?
> Cattle-rearing generates more climate-changing greenhouse gases than all the world's transport put together.
> *Source: UN's Food and Agriculture Organisation*

way than intensively farmed goods. However, imported organics (especially air freighted ones) clock up the food miles so go for produce that is in season and check where it has come from.

- **Fish right** – The World Wildlife Fund (WWF) estimates that 75 per cent of fish stocks are fully or over-exploited, so look for the Marine Stewardship Council (MSC) logo to ensure that you are buying fish that comes from a sustainable source and has been harvested ethically. Most supermarkets stock many MSC accredited products.
- **Eat less meat** – A vegetarian or vegan diet is environmentally better, since meat production uses far more water and generates more greenhouse gases. If you are a meat-eater, have two or three meatless days a week: you might find you want to do it more often.

Above: Organic vegetable boxes cut down on packaging and encourage you to cook with different vegetables.

SHOPPING WITH SENSE

Globally, we create far more waste than we know how to dispose of. In among our mountains of rubbish are many items that could easily have been passed on, or need not have been bought in the first place. Changing the way that you shop will save you pounds and avoid using the world's resources unnecessarily.

General principles

Keep these principles in mind to avoid the temptations of our 'disposable living' culture.

- **Do I need it?** – Before you buy anything, ask yourself why you are spending the money. Resist impulse purchases which simply add to the waste mountain.
- **Buy to last** – Quality goods may cost more but don't have to be replaced as often. Spending more on items such as everyday shoes can save money in the long run.
- **Repair rather than replace** – Many items that are thrown onto landfill need only a simple repair. It's cheaper and more environmentally friendly to mend and keep.
- **Donate or recycle** – If you are replacing an item that still functions (a laptop or a TV set) give the old one away. If it's broken beyond repair, check with your local authority how

to dispose of it, or see the website *www. recycle-more.co.uk* for advice on recycling.

Clothes

As cheap clothing becomes more and more readily available, our attitude towards it has become increasingly wasteful. It has been estimated that the average person spends more than £6,000 in their lifetime on clothes and shoes that are never worn.

- **Plan ahead** – Cut waste by checking your wardrobe and working out exactly what you need before you shop.
- **Think about fabric** – Choose clothes made from sustainable, natural materials – organic cotton or silk, hemp, bamboo and tensel (made from wood pulp cellulose). Choosing organic cotton is particularly important as cotton is a hugely unsustainable industry.
- **Go for recycled goods** – Look out for clothes made from recycled textiles and plastic. Use the internet to find sources near you and be on the lookout at high-street retailers and eco-fashion stores.
- **Make do and mend** – Get shoes re-heeled or re-soled rather than throwing them out. Have a mini repair kit at home so that you can make small repairs yourself.

Furniture and appliances

Three quarters of all electrical appliances end up on landfill where harmful chemicals leach into the environment. Every year we dump 200 million electrical products, including TVs, mobile phones and stereos. Furniture and appliances are also a considerable cost so reducing wastage could save you money too.

- **Refurbish** – Before you replace your sofa, think whether a steam clean or new covers will give it a new lease of life.

- **Go second-hand** – Old furniture is so much more characterful than new – and old things are not always expensive antiques. Look out for shops that sell stripped Victorian pine – it looks good, fits anywhere, and because it has been around for a century or more, it is not depleting the world's forests.

- **Buy from sustainable sources** – Logging is responsible for a third of global deforestation so check that any wooden furniture you buy is made from recycled or reclaimed timber, or comes from a well-managed forest. The Forest Stewardship Council (FSC) certifies wooden products from responsible sources. Look for their label as FSC-certified products are readily available but many stores sell a mixture of certified and non-certified products. See *www.fsc.org* for details.

- **Be energy-efficient** – Always look for the energy-saving label (now compulsory) on fridges, freezers and washing machines. The most energy-efficient models are ranked A (A+ or A++ for fridges and freezers). They are more expensive to buy, but cheaper to run, so can be more economical in the long run.

- **Maintain it** – Taking basic steps to look after your appliances will extend their life, and make them work more efficiently (see pages 16–17, *The Greener Kitchen*). Get your appliances serviced and repaired – replacing a worn seal will be a lot cheaper than buying a new machine.

£ Shop around

Check prices at different retailers and price comparison websites before you buy appliances. Use this information to negotiate a discount at a local shop. If you can't get a discount, ask for free delivery – many retailers will agree to get the sale.

SECOND TIME AROUND

Eschewing the new is one of the best ways of cutting the cost of your goods – both to your pocket and the planet. There are many sources of pre-owned goods and there are also plenty of places that you can get items for free. Hiring and share-purchase are two more green ways to save pounds.

Pre-owned goods

Try some of the following sources for second-hand bargains.

- **Charity shops** – Many people donate unwanted (sometimes unused) clothes and household items to charity shops. The best goods tend to be found in shops in affluent areas. You'll often find dress agencies here as well, selling desirable, high-quality items. They're businesses so the goods will be more expensive than at a charity shop but still much cheaper than buying new.
- **Car boot sales** – Car boot sales are a good place to grab a bargain. They often have a mixture of professional sellers and ordinary people selling their unwanted goods. Garage sales and jumble sales are another good source of pre-owned items.
- **Direct from the seller** – Many people sell their second-hand goods through listings in local papers or via the internet. Look for your free local paper at your newsagent or check out ebay and other auction sites.
- **Police sales** – The police sell off recovered, seized and unwanted goods including bikes, furniture and jewellery when they cannot locate the owner. Bid for items at *www.bumblebeeauctions.co.uk*.
- **Reclamation yards and salvage merchants** – A good source of vintage furnishings, timber and other materials.
- **Auctions** – If you are looking for an item of furniture, check out your local auction house. You get a chance to examine objects before the sale. Consider what your maximum price is before you start to bid – and make sure you stick to it, else the money-saving benefits will be lost.

Sharing goods

Hiring and share-purchase are two more green ways that you can save pounds.

- **Be a borrower** – Before spending money on large DIY items that you are likely to need infrequently, see if you can borrow one. There's no point buying a ladder and wallpaper-paste table that you will need only occasionally if your neighbour is willing to lend you one.

- **Split the cost** – Alternatively, think about buying large infrequently used items with a group of neighbours or friends. For example, if you have good relations with your neighbour, it may make financial sense for you to buy one lawnmower between you.
- **Hire** – Hiring items such as paint strippers is a good way to save money, and avoid adding to future waste mountains.

Getting it for free

t might sound too good to be true but there are even ways that you can get the things you need for free.

- **Join Freecycle** – An online organisation which matches people with something to give away with people who are looking for just that item. (See pages 24–25, *Recycling* for more information and *www.freecycle. org* for details of your local group).
- **Check the skip** – Be on the lookout for items thrown out by people renovating a home. Many people put large items of furniture on the street or in a skip. However, do make sure that you ask permission before you take anything.
- **Throw a swap party** – Known as swishing, clothes swapping allows you to recycle

your unwanted clothes and shoes, and pick up some new ones. It is great fun: everyone brings their unwanted clothes and puts them in a large pile in the centre, then you all rummage through and pick out what you want. See *www.swishing.org* for details and organised events.

Above: Auctions can be good for buying furniture but remember not to get carried away with your bidding.

THE GREEN YOU

Reconsider how you manage your personal life and you can make a big difference to your impact on the planet, your health and your bank balance. It won't take a fundamental difference to your lifestyle; mostly it's about knowing the environmental implications of your daily routines and making the changes that will work for you. Thinking about where energy is spent can reduce your personal expenditure and have both a local and global impact on reducing carbon emissions. Depending on your preferences, it can also help to improve methods of manufacture, give back to local communities and put you in control of how your money is used.

Left: Avocado, oats and honey can all be used to make your own natural bathroom products.

DEJUNK YOUR BATHROOM CABINET

Bathrooms are often stocked up with expensive synthetic beauty and hygiene products, disposable razors, electric razors, electric toothbrushes and more. Rather than being a haven of personal care and pampering, the bathroom contains a cocktail of toxic chemicals and is responsible for some significant CO_2 emissions.

Bathroom CO_2

Most products used in the bathroom are highly processed in their manufacture, packaged in plastic (sometimes several layers) and transported around the world. This adds up to a lot of wasted energy and CO_2 – but it can easily be reduced.

- **Don't impulse buy** – Resist the marketing and avoid buying toiletries and cosmetics on impulse, they are usually the ones that get thrown away. Try out new products with miniature samples.
- **Avoid disposables** – A razor and replacement blades costs about £5.

Natural products and treatments

Many beauty products contain ingredients that are toxic. The amount is minute, but over a number of years they accumulate and can cause health problems. A healthier choice is to buy the natural and organic toiletries and cosmetics sold alongside the chemical-based products – or try making your own.

- **Soap** – The manufacture of palm oil-based soap is leading to devastating deforestation so buy olive oil-based soaps or go to retailers with strict environmental policies.
- **Hair conditioner** – Massage olive oil into hair and then wrap in a warm towel for 30 minutes. Add lemon juice to a mild shampoo and rinse in warm water.
- **Facial treatment** – Mix together an egg yolk, mashed banana and two teaspoons of almond oil. Apply to face and neck for 10 minutes. Rinse off with lukewarm water. Skin will feel soft and deeply moisturised.

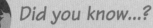

Did you know...?

Changing from an electric to an ordinary toothbrush will save 48g (1.7oz) of CO_2 a day.

Source: United Nations Guide to Climate Neutrality (2008)

- **Body scrub** – Place equal amounts of bran and crushed oats (porridge oats) in a muslin bag and use this to clean yourself under the shower. Oats and bran are natural cleansers and good for exfoliation.
- **Deodorant** – Deodorant crystals are available from health stores. They work by coating the skin surface, without blocking the pores, and eliminating the bacteria that cause body odour.
- **Aftershave** – Diluted witch hazel will close up skin pores after shaving.
- **Toothpaste** – Use natural toothpaste or brush your teeth with bicarbonate of soda.

Hair washing

Shampoo and conditioners contain chemical ingredients such as sodium lauryl sulphate (which is known to be an irritant) plus a host of detergents and preservatives. Hair is just as clean without shampoo and conditioners so you can stop using them altogether, saving yourself money in the process.

- **Just water** – Washing hair in warm water every day removes dust and dirt. After several weeks the hair regains its natural balance and is healthy and shiny.

- **Add vinegar** – To quickly remove shampoo and conditioner residue, rinse hair with vinegar and equal parts warm water.

Feminine hygiene

Manufacture of tampons and sanitary pads has improved but questions remain about the use of bleach and the dangers of toxic shock syndrome. The average woman uses 11,000 pads and tampons in her lifetime – some go into landfill, but 2.5 million tampons a year are flushed into the sewage system.

- **Go organic** – Organic products are free of chemicals and no more expensive.
- **Try alternatives** – Most women spend up to £90 a year on feminine hygiene products. Save money with alternative methods such as menstrual cups and sponges, which are reusable.

£ *Home spa treatment*
Both honey and the flesh of avocados can be used to make home-made face masks allowing you to pamper yourself without the expense of shop-bought products.

GIZMOS AND GADGETS

Gadgets and gizmos are often the latest must-have or just a bit of fun. They can consume a lot of energy and end up in landfill where, as they are invariably made of plastic, they take several lifetimes to break down. However, if you like gadgets and gizmos, there are many ways that you can save energy without giving them up altogether.

Energy-saving plugs

Homes in Britain lose around £4 billion in wasted electricity by leaving appliances on standby. From the television to the microwave clock, kilowatts are ticking away and generating unnecessary CO_2. The most important thing you can do is simply to switch products off and avoid the temptation to leave them on standby. Gadgets that reliably and conveniently shut down appliances can also save you electricity and carbon emissions.

- **Remote control** – For TVs and general appliances there are energy-saving plugs that work by remote control radio frequency with the option to control up to four zones around the house.
- **For computers** – Dedicated computer energy-saving plugs are rather like a

multi-way extension cable. Plug in the desktop computer, your printer and any other associated hardware and it will all shut down automatically when you power down the computer.

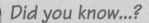

Did you know...?
Every year sound systems on standby cost UK householders £290 million in wasted electricity and produce 1.6 million tonnes of CO_2.
Source: The Energy Saving Trust

Around the house

There are a number of gadgets that can be put to good use around the house.

- **Electricity monitors** – There are two types of these. Simple monitors plug into a wall socket, you then plug the appliance that you wish to check into the meter and it displays the electricity usage and cost of the appliance in use. More sophisticated monitors can be attached to your electricity meter and connect wirelessly to a reader telling you how much energy you are using overall, how much it is costing you and even how much carbon dioxide is being produced. Some models even glow red or blue if your average consumption varies. It has the effect of sending everyone running to turn off appliances.

- **Eco-kettle** – A green kettle boils only as many cups of water as required and a single cup takes just three seconds to boil.
- **Old-fashioned alarm** – Instead of using an electric alarm clock, or your mobile phone to wake you up, get a windup alarm clock.
- **Shower timer** – Control shower water consumption with a waterproof timer. Fixed with a suction pad, the timer is adjustable and there is a built-in alarm.

Batteries

So many gadgets are battery powered, causing around 600 million 12 volt batteries to be dumped in landfill every year – that equates in weight to 110 jumbo jets. Most batteries contain mercury and cadmium, which can be recycled and shouldn't be left to leach into the ground. Recycling is a priority but there are other options as well.

- **Recharge** – Rechargeable batteries are the best option. They save on waste and it is also much cheaper than continually buying replacement batteries.

above: Wireless electricity monitors have been shown to lead to a self-imposed drop in electricty usage.

ETHICAL FINANCE

Most people don't know where their money is going when they invest or deposit it. But for concerned investors, there are ethical and socially responsible options that ensure that your money is not being used to fund business that you find unacceptable.

Ethical investment

Now a significant part of the banking world, ethical funds can perform just as well as other funds. Investors should consult a qualified financial adviser before taking any financial decisions. Investments are screened, positively and negatively.

- **Negative screening** – Might exclude armaments and oppressive regimes; pharmaceuticals, GM products, tobacco and alcohol manufacture; activities that harm the environment and animal testing.

Did you know...?

In 1989 the amount of money invested in ethical investment funds was under £200 million. By 1999 it was almost £2.5 billion and by the end of 2007, just under £9 billion.
Source: Ethical Investment Research Service (2008 report)

- **Positive screening** – Supports investment in areas such as renewable energy; inner city regeneration, transport solutions and companies promoting policies of employee welfare and environmental management.
- **Engagement** – Engagement is using the funds' influence over companies to encourage them to adopt higher standards of corporate responsibility (such as improving conditions for workers) or change their behaviour (such as pulling out investment from oppressive regimes). Many think it's a more effective way to influence companies' behaviour than simple screening processes.

Ethical banking and saving

High street banks with an ethical mandate are limited in the UK but many banks have adopted ethical policies in some areas of business. See the free buyers' guide on *www.ethicalconsumer.org* for an independent rating.

- **Credit cards** – There are now credit cards which donate profits to environmental or charitable projects or give a better rate of interest for approved ethical companies.
- **Ethical savings accounts** – Available from some high street banks (can include ISAs).

£ Think incentives

Government incentive schemes offer tax relief on a five-year investment plan in not-for-profit organisations via a Community Development Finance Institution (CDFI). Investing £10,000 would entitle the investor to tax relief worth £500 each year for five years.

Ethical mortgages and pensions

Some high street mortgage lenders have ethical lending policies, others specialise in socially and environmentally responsible funding or will take measures to offset the impact of CO_2 from homes.

Pensions – UK pension funds have to disclose if they incorporate ethical considerations into how they invest the pension holder's funds.

Lending – Specialist lenders offer mortgages for property in need of substantial repair and to housing co-operatives and self-build projects.

Ethical insurance

Insurance companies are some of the biggest institutional investors in the world so they are often the same companies that you trust your investments to. Some insurance companies apply ethical criteria to their investment decisions, but it is difficult for individual investors to assess their claims.

- **Find an ethical insurer** – Ethical Consumer magazine have a free report on insurance companies on their website (*www.ethicalconsumer.org*).
- **Green policies** – Switch to an insurer that offsets CO_2 on an individual basis according to model of car, annual mileage or distance to a holiday destination. Some insurers offer discounts of up to 15 per cent on hybrid cars and cars running on alternative fuels such as LPG.

Advice on ethical finance

Before making any financial decisions, seek the advice of an independent financial adviser (IFA) with experience of ethical finance.

- **Find an IFA** – See the Ethical Investment Research Service (*www.eiris.org*) or the Ethical Investment Association (*www. ethicalinvestment.org.uk*).
- **Decide your preferences** – Consider your personal preferences (areas of business you want to avoid or support) and what risks (if any) you are prepared to take.

THE GREEN FAMILY

Britain has 12 million children under the age of 16 and the estimated cost of bringing up a child is £50,000, so it's not surprising that the family market is such an important one for so many industries. Countless marketing campaigns try to attract our hard-earned cash regardless of whether the product is good for the child or the planet. Resisting the pressure isn't always easy but making informed decisions about the things we buy for our families and how we feed and care for them can have a far-reaching impact on bank balance, global warming and the volume of landfill.

For many families, especially those with working parents, time is a problem, but a shift in routine can sometimes allow us to slow down a little and consider how the whole family can make a difference and reduce their environmental impact.

Left: Encouraging your children to appreciate nature will help to ensure that they adopt an eco-friendly lifestyle.

BABY EQUIPMENT

The essence of a greener approach is reducing the amount of 'stuff' that we buy. There is a lot of pressure to have a well-equipped nursery and the cost of the basic equipment for a first baby starts at £1,500 with the average spend considerably more – and that doesn't include clothes, nappies or any consumables.

What does a baby really need?

Drawing up a list of the essentials will help to avoid unnecessary spending especially as most first babies are inundated with presents from friends and family. If you do want to invest in larger items, such as a pram travel system (see below), ask friends and relatives to contribute towards the cost instead.

- **Somewhere to sleep** – A crib or Moses basket is very short term and a baby can go into a cot straight away, saving around £100. A quilted sleeping bag will keep the baby feeling snug and secure.
- **Going out** – Buying a pram, a pushchair and a sling could set you back around £500. Instead get a pram travel system that allows the baby to lie down and converts to a seat when he/she is big enough. This will save £150 or more. A baby sling only costs

around £35 and can be invaluable for the first few months.

- **Changing** – A changing station is convenient but costs from £150 upwards and a thick towel on top of a chest of drawers will do just as well. Or keep it simple and change your baby on the floor.
- **Washing** – A baby bath reduces the amount of water needed for bathing, but babies soon outgrow them. The basin is a good alternative, saving about £20.
- **Travelling** – It is essential to keep your baby safe and secure when travelling by car. A travel seat will cost around £80 but many pram systems include a detachable travel seat.

Sourcing baby equipment

It's hard to resist buying everything new for a first baby. Equipment can be used for subsequent children but, for most items, it makes green sense to swap and share equipment with friends and family or to buy second-hand.

- **Sales** – Make the most of sales held by antenatal groups.
- **Ebay** – Search through ebay or other internet auction sites for sales of baby equipment. Make sure, however, that you

£ Think alternatives
Versatile baby equipment and
avoiding short-term purchases
can save more than £500.

know the history of the product, have a copy of the instructions (if installation is required), that the product meets the most recent safety standards and that it is hygienic or can be thoroughly cleaned.

- **Local papers** – Use the For Sale and Wanted columns of your local newspaper.
- **Freecycle** – Register with your local group of Freecycle, the online recycling network. (See pages 24–25 for more information and *www.freecycle.org* for details of your local Freecycle group).

Brand new equipment

If you're buying new baby equipment, it is worth considering the carbon footprint of what you're buying.

- **Less miles** – Look for UK or European manufacture and reduce the emissions from transporting goods around the world.
- **Avoid plastic and PVC** – These are very slow to break down so your equipment will end up in a landfill site, probably for several

centuries. There are also serious health concerns about PVC in baby products.

- **Go for wood** – Cots, highchairs and changing stations made of wood cost about the same as the plastic versions, they last longer and are biodegradable.

Above: Look for quality, sustainably produced wooden furniture – better still, buy it second-hand.

NATURAL BABYCARE

Products for babies and children, especially skincare products, are specially formulated, but there is still some concern about the amount of chemicals they contain and whether there is any long-term health hazard. Natural materials and skincare preparations are one way to avoid this.

Sun protection

Exposure to the sun is especially dangerous for children as they have much thinner skin than adults. Damage done at an early age may not be evident until later in life.

- **Be careful** – Cover up and keep out of the sun between 11am and 3pm to reduce the amount of sun cream used.
- **Go natural** – Natural and organic sun creams use naturally occurring minerals to filter out UV rays and plant extracts to protect the skin from free-radicals. With chemical filters used in traditional sun cream threatening the world's coral reefs, they are also kinder to the environment.

Dealing with nits

Head lice cause skin irritation and an allergic reaction in susceptible people. The chemical base of over-the-counter treatments brings its own problems and with children aged 4–11 most at risk, there are concerns about overexposure to chemicals.

- **Insecticides** – Over-the-counter treatments have insecticides as the active ingredient. These can cause skin irritations. Studies show Permethrin 1% to be the most effective treatment but many strains of head lice are becoming resistant.
- **Prevention** – The Department of Health recommends regular checking and 'bug busting' to keep infestations at bay. Coat the hair in conditioner and take a fine-tooth comb (nit comb) through every section to remove any lice and eggs. Each session takes about 30 minutes.
- **Natural options** – There are a number of natural preparations available using herbs and oils, particularly tea tree oil. Most of these work on the basis of making the scalp unattractive to head lice.

The nappy debate

From birth to toilet training, a baby will need about 5,300 changes of nappy. An updated Environment Agency study released in 2007 concluded that the environmental benefit of cloth nappies over disposables can be considerable but only if they are washed

for 20, organic cotton terry squares cost £66 for 20. Two-part nappies cost from £190 for 20 and all-in-ones cost around £285 for 20. Biodegradable nappy liners, odour-proof bucket and cleansing solution will cost around £100 from start to finish. The Real Nappy exchange puts you in touch with people with equipment to pass on (*www.realnappiesforlondon.org.uk*).

n an energy-efficient machine, with full oads, at low temperatures and line dried.

- **Disposable nappies** – Disposable nappies for one child from birth to toilet training cost between £800 and £1,000 depending on the brand. Made largely from synthetic materials, they take upwards of 200 years to decompose and there are health concerns about the chemicals and adhesives they contain.

- **Biodegradable disposables** – Cost slightly more than conventional disposables but are made from plant-based materials. However, there is not enough air in landfill sites for them to biodegrade and this results in the release of methane which is a worse greenhouse gas than CO_2.

- **Cloth nappies** – Last through at least two babies. Cotton terry squares plus nappy ties and waterproof outers cost around £50

£ Go fabric

Using terry or cloth nappies from birth to toilet training can save you between £500 and £700 and reduce the volume of long-term landfill.

Source: Environment Agency and Women's Environmental Network (WEN)

Disposable wipes

Wipes are also expected to take centuries to decompose in landfill. Made from man-made fibres, they can contain Propylene glycol, an ingredient in anti-freeze.

- **Washable wipes** – Cost about £5 for ten. With disposable wipes costing around £2 a pack, the reuse will soon save you money.

- **Organic wipes** – These are made with natural fibres and ingredients.

TOYS AND CLOTHES

Keeping children dressed and occupied with toys comes at an ever-increasing cost financially, environmentally and ethically. Cutting down on the quantity of new clothes and toys that you buy will reduce the carbon footprint of manufacture and transport, and slow down the rate of landfill.

Second-hand clothes

If everyone in Britain used one recycled jumper instead of buying new, it would save more than the water in an average reservoir (300 million gallons) and around 480 tonnes of chemical dyes.

- **Look online** – Online auction sites are a good source of quality children's clothes.
- **Browse charity shops** – Often have a good range of children's clothes and toys.
- **Pass it on** – Become a seller as well as a buyer of outgrown toys and clothes.

Back to school

Lots of schools have specific sweatshirts or jumpers that can be bought direct, but otherwise you can shop around for the best options – although many garments have a poor ethical source and a large carbon footprint from transport.

- **Think Fairtrade** – Some high street retailers have Fairtrade school uniforms that costs no more than other ranges.
- **Chemicals to avoid** – Avoid garments that contain fluoropolymers. These are chemicals that make the fabric harder wearing but they can be absorbed by the body and these coated fabrics don't break down in landfill.
- **Second-hand** – Many schools have second-hand uniform shops, often run by the PTA. They are a reliable source of good quality and nearly new uniforms.
- **Green stationery** – Get ready for studying with recycled paper, wooden gel pens and pencils that are certified by the Forest Stewardship Council (FSC).
- **Recycled products** – There are a wide range of recycled products available, from pencil cases to backpacks made from water bottles and recycled packaging.

Toys

Plastic toys are often cheap but, depending on the composition, there can be a high price to pay in terms of their carbon footprint. PVC plastics (polyvinyl chloride) release toxins throughout the stages of manufacture, during use and right up to disposal.

Wooden toys – These are often no more expensive than plastic, they last for years and they are non-toxic and biodegradable.

Keep their interest – Putting some toys away from time to time can stop children getting bored of them.

Greener plastic – When buying plastic toys look for recycled plastic or toys that are labelled PVC-free. Toys made from Polypropylene (PP) and Polyethylene (PE) are less harmful to the environment and safer for your child.

Toy libraries

Toy libraries have good-quality toys and activity play equipment that can be loaned, making them the perfect solution to keeping children stimulated without spending lots of money on new toys that they'll get bored of quickly. They also save on storage space as toys can take over a small house. There are more than 1,000 toy libraries in Britain.

• **Charges** – Loan periods are usually two weeks and costs about 20p per item – some libraries don't charge at all.

• **Information** – To find a nearby toy library ask at your local library or contact the National Association of Toy and Leisure Libraries (*www.natll.org.uk*). Contact details are on their website and if you have your postcode ready, they'll tell you where to find your nearest registered toy library.

Toy swap
Borrowing two toys each month
for a year will provide lots of
interest and cost less then £5.

Above: Wooden toys are greener, look more pleasant and will last longer.

FOOD AND DRINK FOR KIDS

Feeding children can be difficult and ensuring a balanced diet that is environmentally sound can feel like an uphill struggle for busy parents. Making just one change at a time will encourage healthier eating habits and cut down on waste and CO_2 emissions.

First foods

Baby food in jars is very convenient and you can buy organic foods that are excellent. But they are expensive and invariably there is some wastage of food (the manufacturers recommend any food left over is thrown away) – and then there are all those jars.

- **Make your own** – Make your own weaning foods (such as mashed potato or carrot) and freeze them in baby-sized portions – an ice cube mould is about the right size.
- **Meals to go** – Small size freezer boxes are really useful for taking meals out with you

or supplying meals for nursery care. Some nurseries are concerned about reheating chicken so this is best avoided.

- **Share yours** – As babies get older and their tastes widen, try puréed small portions of your own food. Don't cook with salt – it's better for you too.

School lunches

Lunch boxes of ready-prepared foods can be a horror story of processed foods with little nutritional value and lots of plastic packaging. Processed foods are high in sugar, salts and saturated fats which boost blood sugar and then result in a big energy let-down. Wholegrain breads and fresh fruit and vegetables will maintain energy levels.

£ *Avoid those jars*
A week's supply of two savouries and a dessert per day in manufactured baby food will cost over £20. Making your own baby food will cost less than £5.

Above: Sending your child to school with a healthy, filling lunch will help them to resist junk snacks

- **Go for variety** – Keep the lunch box interesting with varied breads and fillings. Add salads, carrot sticks and cherry tomatoes and try rice or pasta salad for variety. Include fruits in season and maybe nuts, raisins and low-sugar cereal bars.
- **Lunch boxes** – Use a recycled plastic lunch box, some are moulded into trays designed to contain different foods and avoid additional packaging.
- **Refillable plastic containers** – These can be used for yoghurts and fruit salads.
- **Stainless steel drinks bottle** – Refilling one of these will help to reduce the 10 billion plastic bottles going into landfill every year and protect your child from any effects of drinking from plastic bottles.
- **Sandwiches** – Make sandwiches and wrap them in greaseproof paper or put them in a reusable plastic box.

Party food

Children's birthday parties can be very stressful and feeding them crisps, sausage rolls, cakes and fizzy drinks will probably increase the hyperactivity factor.

- **Popular options** – Not all children will eat carrot sticks and healthy sandwiches but keep it simple and colourful. Try pizza

> ### Did you know...?
> A litre of tap water costs just 0.22 pence – 141 times cheaper than a litre of bottled water.
> *Source: Which?*

slices, smoothies, chicken drumsticks, sausages, dips, filled pitta bread, fruit juice.

- **Under fives** – A lunch party is best for under fives – they are usually at their best at this time and lunch followed by birthday cake makes life so much simpler.

Pick your own and foraging

For families who can't grow their own fruit and vegetables, a visit to a pick-your-own farm can be really good fun and helps children to understand where fruit and vegetables come from and to appreciate their seasonal nature.

- **Not just fruit** – Soft fruits are the most popular pick-your-own produce but peas and beans are good too and children love popping the pea pods.
- **Go wild** – Go for a country walk in autumn and collect blackberries from field hedgerows. Avoid roadside berries which are subject to car exhaust fumes.

GREEN CELEBRATIONS

Many celebrations, especially Christmas, have become something of a consumer frenzy with a fortune spent on gifts and food that are often wasted. Changes can be made that reduce the environmental impact of all our celebrations – they can be just as special and less expensive.

Parties and picnics

Shopping for a party often involves a big supermarket shop and lots of packaging and rubbish. Making your party greener will reduce waste and save you money.

- **Avoid plastic cups and plates** – Recycled paper cups, plates and cutlery for parties and picnics will save washing up and can be recycled again or composted.
- **Bottles and cans** – Should be recycled.

Weddings

For most people a wedding is the biggest celebration they will ever have, with a carbon footprint to match. Two airline tickets and 150 wedding guests represent about 14.5 tonnes of CO_2 – four tonnes more than the average annual footprint of one person. Green weddings are the new white – no less stylish, cheaper and environmentally friendly.

- **Less car travel** – Keep the service and reception as close as possible and encourage guests to take public transport or car share.
- **Flowers** – Most florists' flowers are imported. Use native flowers in season.
- **Think local** – Plan a wedding breakfast that uses local produce.
- **UK honeymoon** – This cuts your air miles.

Christmas cards

The UK sends over 700 million Christmas cards and most of these go to landfill.

- **Go electronic** – Email cards will convey the sentiment (if not the tradition).
- **Make your cards from last year's** – Helps to reduce the 250,000 trees cut down annually for Christmas cards.
- **Charity cards on recycled paper** – Cost from as little as 25p. Buy from the charity shop for maximum return to the charity.
- **Recycle cards** – See the Woodland Trust website (*www.woodland-trust.org.uk*).

Christmas decorations

Decorating your home at Christmas need not be at the expense of the environment.

- **Reuse last year's** – You can always ring the changes with coloured ribbon bows.

- **Christmas biscuits** – Make a hole in your biscuit before it is baked, thread through ribbon or string when the biscuits are cold, decorate with icing to make them pretty and hang on the tree.
- **The holly and the ivy** – Use greenery from the garden to decorate the house.
- **Shred it** – Many local authorities will collect Christmas trees for shredding.

Christmas presents

For many people, the Christmas gift exchange has got out of hand, involving lots of expense, waste and unwanted presents.

- **Cut down on packaging** – It all goes to landfill – and it can account for 25–50 per cent of the value of the gift.
- **Make a list** – Christmas lists ensure nobody receives presents they don't want, reducing wasted, unwanted presents.
- **Ethical gifts** – For people who have everything they want, make a gift of livestock to a developing nation.

Christmas dinner

The UK consumes more than 10 million turkeys at Christmas with frozen turkeys coming from as far away as Thailand, clocking up transport emissions on the way.

- **Buy local** – Buy a fresh local turkey that is the right size for your family and help to reduce the 160,000 tonnes of food waste that goes into landfill after Christmas. Alternatively, try a vegetarian Christmas.

£ *Make your own*
Homemade cards cost around 5p–8p for card and envelope. For every 20 cards you send, that's a saving of £3–£4 or more.

Above: Hanging decorations in a new place makes them look different so you can reuse last year's.

CHOOSING A GREEN FUNERAL

Eco-friendly lifestyle changes to improve the health of the planet can go beyond changing our daily habits to reduce our carbon footprint. Conventional funerals are far from eco-friendly and recognition of this has meant that the number of people opting for a green funeral is increasing at a steady rate and is predicted to be 12 per cent of all burials by 2010.

What is a green funeral?

Essentially it is the environmentally friendly disposal of human remains and usually consists of a burial in a woodland or meadow setting using a biodegradable coffin and without preserving the body with embalming chemicals. Whether you arrange a green funeral yourself or engage a funeral director, the costs are considerably lower than a traditional burial or cremation.

- **Legal requirements** – These are more concerned with health and safety than the niceties of convention or religion.
- **Service** – Can include as much or as little of a conventional funeral service as you like.
- **Cost** – The average cost of a basic conventional funeral is £1,300–£2,000, plus the cost of a plot if it is a burial. Depending on what is included, the cost of a green burial is around 30 per cent of that of a conventional funeral that uses the services of a funeral director.
- **Emissions** – 70 per cent of UK funerals are cremation, resulting in an increase of polluting mercury emissions caused by the melting of dental fillings.

Green burial grounds

There are over 200 green burial sites in Britain. The majority are owned by local authorities, about 30 per cent are privately owned and around a dozen are run by charitable or not-for-profit organisations. The coffins used are more rapidly biodegradable and the grave is typically marked by planting a tree.

- **The coffin** – Green coffins are usually made from willow, wicker, bamboo or cardboard. A cardboard coffin costs from £55. Made from recycled materials it can take a weight of 108kg (17 stone).
- **Reduced fees** – Some local authorities will reduce the cremation fees at the crematorium when a green coffin is used.
- **Break down time** – A traditional oak coffin takes 50 years to break down.

DIY funeral

It is possible to carry out a funeral without involving a funeral director, providing the legal requirements of a death certificate and registering the death have been followed. There is also no legal requirement that a burial takes place in a designated burial ground but the chosen site must comply with regulations to ensure there is no health risk.

- **Location** – Legally you can even choose your back garden providing it complies with regulations. However, a designated burial ground is more likely to ensure there is no disruption to the grave site.
- **Advice** – The charitable organisation The Natural Death Centre (*www. naturaldeath.org.uk*) publishes a resource list and will advise on arranging a low-cost conventional or green funeral.

Religious services

This is something for discussion with your religious or spiritual adviser but religious involvement in a green funeral is becoming more commonplace. A religious green funeral might include a church service before the burial tales place and then a blessing of the burial site or just a blessing. The usual clergy fees will be required.

- **Spiritual** – For a spiritual but non-religious funeral, the Humanist Association have a helpline and a searchable database *www.humanism.org.uk*.

Burial at sea

This is more restricted and, although it is possible to organise without the help of professionals, it is a more complicated process and requires notice to the coroner and a special licence granted by the Department for Environment, Food and Rural Affairs (DEFRA). In the UK there are around 15 sea burials each year.

- **Costs** – A funeral director will charge £2,000–£3,000 to arrange a burial at sea.
- **Sites** – There are two sea burial sites in the UK. The Needles Spoil Ground to the west of the Isle of Wight and another off the coast at Newhaven, East Sussex.

Above: Willow coffins are available in many designs and are a good green option.

THE GREEN WORKPLACE

Many of the energy-saving measures for the home are just as effective in the workplace. Whether in offices, workshops or on the factory floor, it is estimated that Britain could save 11 million tonnes of CO_2 and £1.4 billion by adopting energy-saving measures that are mostly just common sense and good business practice. Simple steps like turning off the lights, powering down computers and equipment when they're not in use, printing both sides of the paper or not printing at all, will all go a long way towards making significant savings on overheads. A review of factors such as transport, travel, energy consumption and waste management enables businesses to put in place an Environmental Management System (EMS) that will cut costs and reduce CO_2 emissions.

Left: Even simple measures like taking the stairs and not the lift can reduce your carbon footprint.

EQUIPMENT AND SUPPLIES

Cutting energy consumption and reducing the carbon footprint of your business will save money and reduce CO$_2$ emissions. The first step is to assess the carbon footprint of your business and audit energy consumption over a standard working week.

Energy audit

To do your own audit, walk around the workplace and note equipment in use, any equipment not used regularly, settings on the heating system and any other energy consumption. Make a note of meter readings at the start and end of the working day. Alternatively you can hire a energy auditor, many give free consultations.

- **Calculate your carbon footprint** – Go to *www.carbontrust.co.uk/footprintcalculator* – you will need information such as your electricity bills and vehicle use.

£ **Shut down to save**
Switch off computers when not in use – powering just one PC only when it is needed can save £35 per year.
Source: The Energy Saving Trust

- **Out of hours** – Monitoring the out of hours consumption will show how much electricity the business is consuming from equipment left plugged in or on standby.
- **Grants** – These are available to businesses implementing major energy reductions. (See *www.lowcarbonbuildings.org.uk*).

Reducing consumption

With your energy audit results, you are now in a better position to put maximum energy saving measures in place. Continue to monitor your electricity consumption to find out exactly how much you are saving – it will really motivate you.

- **Don't leave anything on standy** – Be sure to switch off equipment that is not in use. Leaving equipment on standby uses almost as much energy as having it on.
- **Fit timers** – Timers can be fitted to water coolers and vending machines.
- **Use low energy** – Check that all light bulbs are low energy.
- **Turn it down** – Reducing the heating by one degree and setting it to turn off half an hour before the end of the working day can save eight per cent of your heating cost.
- **Monitor your meter reading** – A great motivator for reducing energy consumption.

Right: Using recycled paper and notepads is one very easy step to a greener workplace.

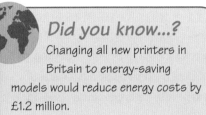

Did you know...?
Changing all new printers in Britain to energy-saving models would reduce energy costs by £1.2 million.

Source: The Energy Saving Trust

Energy-efficient equipment

When renewing equipment, replacing it with energy-efficient models may cost more but will result in lower operating costs. However, the cost and carbon footprint of manufacture can outweigh the benefits of replacing still functioning equipment.

- **Choose flat screens** – They use about half the energy of monitors.
- **Reuse ink cartridges** – Choose a printer that accepts recycled or refillable ink cartridges. It'll cut your overheads as well as CO_2 emissions and the landfill impact.
- **Use laptops** – They are more energy efficient than desktop computers.

Reuse and recycle

The workplace generates a lot of wastage and the growing mountain of discarded IT equipment has led to government legislation on the responsibility for its disposal.

- **Computers disposal** – Under the EU Waste Electrical and Electronic Equipment Directive (WEEE), if a business is replacing (like-for-like) equipment bought before 13 August 2005, then the supplier is responsible for disposal. Otherwise the business user must arrange responsible disposal through an approved waste contractor or WEEE treatment facility. Alternatively, recycle them using Freecycle or charities (see *www.computeraid.org*).
- **Get a reusable cup** – Some coffee shops sell insulated ones with lids.
- **Print double-sided** – Also keep a box of single-sided print for reuse.
- **Recycle** – Arrange with your local authority or waste contractor for recycling bins and bags for paper, cardboard and plastic. It's a legal requirement for you or your waste contractor to pre-sort your rubbish and dispose separately of hazardous waste.
- **Save from the skip** – Metals (e.g. copper) have scrap value, other materials (timber, textiles or rubble) could be recycled.

THE PAPERLESS OFFICE

A completely paperless office is not achievable or even appropriate for many businesses but cutting down on paper use is beneficial. It reduces the use of natural resources and destruction of natural habitats so reducing global warming – and frees you up from dealing with paper documents and records.

Think before you print

Rethinking the need for printing can make the biggest contribution to the paperless office. The average office worker prints out an estimated 1,500 sheets of paper each month, most of which is discarded within two days and often reprinted again. It adds up to a total of 120 billion pages being printed every year in the UK, amounting to 4.7 million tonnes of waste paper and board.

- **Go electronic** – Rather than printing, circulate documents by email instead.
- **Check your settings** – When printing emails, check your settings to avoid printing any more than is necessary.
- **Use double-sided** – Set your printer to print both sides of the paper.
- **Reuse single-side printed paper** – Can be used for printing or as scrap paper.

Paperless fax

As with junk mail, it is actually illegal to send junk fax to a company that has stated its preference not to receive unsolicited faxes. Reducing junk mail will save not only wasting paper but also unnecessary waste of toner, energy and time in dealing with it.

- **Opt out** – Register with the fax preference service to avoid receiving junk faxes (*www.fpsonline.org.uk*). It takes about 28 days to take effect.
- **Use a computer** – Avoid paper waste altogether by receiving and sending faxes from a computer.
- **No cover sheet** – Reduce paper wastage by not using a covering front page when sending a fax.

> *Did you know...?*
> Switching to recycled paper saves 17 trees, 35,000 litres (7,000 gallons) of water, 1,900 litres (380 gallons) of oil, 4,000kWs of energy and three cubic metres (106 cubic feet) of landfill space per tonne.
> *Source: Department for Environment, Food and Rural Affairs (DEFRA) and Envirowise*

Digital storage

Most businesses are required to keep accessible records for many years. Some have more documentation than others, and maintaining those paper records is time consuming and takes up a vast amount of storage space. A digital storage system will significantly cut paper use and reduce the need for paper archives.

- **Keep track** – Digital storage systems create an audit trail of documents.
- **Security** – Allows secure nominated access that can be restricted as required.
- **Scan it** – A scanner can be used for the addition of paper documents. Sensitive documents can be shredded and recycled.

Reducing post

For many businesses, reducing the amount of paper they generate is only half the problem – reducing the quantity of paper delivered by the postman is a significant part of paper handling.

- **Junk mail** – You can't put a stop to all junk mail to a business address but if you're being bombarded by a particular company, contact them and ask them to stop.
- **Electronic bills and invoices** – Arrange with suppliers and clients to send and

Save with Envirowise

Register with Envirowise (*www.envirowise.gov.uk*), the government-funded free advisory service on sustainable and profitable business practice. It saves each of its registered companies an average of £5,000 a year.

Source: Envirowise

receive invoices and statements electronically, including utility bills.

- **Bank online** – Set up online banking for day-to-day transactions and transfers.
- **Circulate publications** – Cancel multiple subscriptions to magazines and journals and set up an internal circulation list.

Above: The more you do electronically and the less you print, the tidier and greener your workplace will be.

THE GREEN LUNCH

Around 22 million adults buy lunch every working day from one source or another. Most of this food is packaged in plastic or foil that ends up in a landfill site. At the same time, food to the value of £10 billion is thrown away every year, creating damaging methane gas. A green approach can reduce the impact of this and save you quite a considerable amount of money.

Bring your own lunch

Making a lunchbox quickly becomes routine. It is a much cheaper option than buying lunch and you know exactly what it contains. Lunch doesn't have to be just sandwiches and by providing your own you are limited only by what is transportable.

- **Eat salads** – Take vegetable salads in a reusable box – carry salad dressing separately to avoid soggy lettuce.
- **Use carbohydrates** – Make more filling salads with pasta, rice or couscous.
- **Try pitta breads** – With a variety of fillings.
- **Use a flask** – Take hot food in a wide-neck flask. The food will keep hot for three to four hours. Fresh soup is a nutritious and satisfying lunch, especially in winter, and a good way of using leftovers.

Reducing waste

Lunchtime and snack food from sandwich bars and supermarkets is individually packaged, mostly in plastic containers, and then put in a plastic bag. Less than five per cent of this is recycled, leaving tonnes of lunchtime rubbish going into landfill sites.

- **Use refillable containers** – Avoid the use of cling film and aluminium foil.
- **Have your own cup** – Cut down on plastic and card waste by using refillable coffee cups and water glasses. Drink tapwater to reduce the massive carbon emissions from providing the UK with bottled water.
- **Avoid highly packaged items** – Avoid buying fruit juice cartons, water in bottles, plastic yoghurt pots and foil crisp packets. Decanting into smaller reusable containers will save money, CO_2 and landfill.

The workplace kitchen

Many small to medium-sized companies have a kitchen. This allows employees to eat more healthily and enjoy the benefits of a more varied diet without spending a lot of money on packaged sandwiches.

- **Equipment** – The ideal workplace kitchen has a sink with hot and cold water, fridge, kettle, toaster and microwave.

£ Bring your own

A recent survey found that British workers spend £5.5 billion on lunches each year, on average spending £3.30 each day. Making your own lunch could save you more than £15 each week.

Source: Waste and Resources Action Programme (WRAP)

- **Leftovers** – For a no-cost, hot, well-balanced lunch, reheat leftovers from home and reduce the methane created from waste food in landfill. Leftover food should be consumed within two days.
- **Eco-kettles** – Save energy with an eco-kettle that boils a single cup of water. If you don't have an eco-kettle, just put the amount you need on to boil.

- **Follow the seasons** – If they don't already, encourage the management to buy local food in season.
- **Have a cooked lunch** – A cooked lunch can be healthy and saves on packaging compared with buying sandwiches.
- **Choose salad** – Salad bars are a good way to have your five-a-day.

The corporate cafeteria

Some larger companies have on-site canteen facilities which are often quite heavily subsidised and offer food options from sandwiches and snacks to breakfast and a three-course lunch. If you can't bring your own lunch, food prepared on-site is the greenest option as it reduces transit miles.

Did you know...?

Every year Britain throws away 2.1 million tonnes of food that could be used for a packed lunch.

Source: Waste and Resources Action Programme (WRAP)

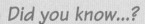

Above: Taking a packed lunch to work encourages you to eat more healthily, reduces packaging and saves money.

BUSINESS TRAVEL

The CO_2 emissions from vehicles transporting people around Britain total around 87 million tonnes each year and at the current rate will increase by 50 per cent by 2026. Carbon emissions from vehicles and aircraft are significant contributors to climate change but small changes can make a difference.

Company cars

Company cars account for the majority of new cars on the road and are responsible for 20 per cent of traffic. That's a major investment for companies and a large contribution to CO_2 emissions. Making the use of company cars more effective reduces the cost and the environmental impact.

- **Go green** – Opt for energy-efficient vehicles or alternative fuel. Keep vehicles serviced for optimal performance.
- **Eco-drive** – Encourage drivers to check tyre pressure regularly, avoid heavy acceleration and breaking, stay below 70mph and clear out unnecessary loads. Eco-driving can save £220 a year per car.

Air travel

Worldwide travel has become an everyday occurrence for many businesses. Accounting for 6.3 per cent of UK CO_2 emissions, air travel has become a major cost for both business budgets and the environment.

- **Use technology** – Avoid travel by holding a conference call or video conference.

- **Go direct** – Avoid changing flights. Take-off and landing use more fuel and create more emissions than cruising flight.

Carbon offset

It is important not to use offsetting as a justification for flying if it is not absolutely necessary. However, if for your business, travel can be reduced but not avoided altogether, you might consider alleviating the environmental effects of your travel by investing in a carbon offsetting scheme (see pages 46–47, *The Flying Issue* for advice on accredited schemes). You can calculate the

Above: Make one conference call instead of travelling to a meeting to save an average 40kg of CO_2.

Did you know...?

A return flight from London to New York generates as much CO_2 as driving a car for four months.

Source: Global Action Plan

carbon footprint of your business travel at Transport Direct (*www.transportdirect.info*).

Car sharing

The majority of drivers commuting to work are the sole occupants of the car. This results in high driving costs and CO_2 emissions, congested roads and a greater need for car parking.

- **National car-sharing network** – Register with a car-sharing organisation (see *www.liftshare.com* for example).
- **Internal car-sharing register** – Set up an internal car-sharing register for your company either as a simple database or using specialist software.
- **Sharing within companies** – Many company cars arrive at the workplace and are then used only occasionally – make use of a corporate car sharing organisation for meetings away from the office.

Transport options

Half the population of Britain lives within walking distance of a railway station and the majority have a bus route nearby. Public transport is much more energy efficient than driving – a 15 mile journey by train emits 1.5kg of CO_2; in a bus it is 2.6kg and in a small car it is 3.1kg.

- **Get a scooter** – If public transport isn't an option and you don't need to carry passengers, replace the car with an electric scooter. They have a lower carbon footprint than petrol-driven models, are cheap to insure and are exempt from road tax and congestion charging.
- **Get a bike** – Cycling to work has the lowest carbon footprint of any form of transport, it's free and it keeps you fit.
- **Take the stairs** – Travelling by lift from the ground to the 4th floor four times a day creates 3kg of CO_2 emissions every week.

£ Get informed

Register with the Energy Saving Trust for free advice on cutting fuel costs and mileage. (See *www.energysavingtrust.org.uk/transport-in-business*).

HOME VS OFFICE

More than 3.4 million people work from home – that's about 12 per cent of the workforce not commuting to their workplace and creating CO_2 emissions. Some of this gain is cancelled out by increased energy use for heating the home, but energy-saving measures can make home working an eco-friendly alternative.

Energy saving

Working from home shifts the energy consumption from a shared working environment to usually just one person. This can increase your working carbon footprint. Taking steps to conserve energy will help to keep down bills and reduce your carbon footprint.

- **Think about suppliers** – Compare energy suppliers and consider switching to a green tariff or renewable energy supplier.
- **Use thermostats** – To make energy savings on daytime heating, fit programmable thermostats around the house so that the home office can be centrally heated without heating all of the house.
- **Go energy saving** – Use low-energy light bulbs and energy-saving plugs.
- **Switch it off** – Never leave any equipment on standby.
- **Get an eco-kettle** – This will avoid using energy to boil water unnecessarily.

Hidden benefits

As well as the reduction in cost and carbon emissions due to reduced travel, there are other ways in which the homeworker reduces their carbon footprint.

- **Cut down on suits** – Home working reduces the need for a smart wardrobe. The selection of dedicated work clothes can be reduced to a few suits and outfits. This saves not only the capital expenditure but the costs and carbon footprint of so much laundry and dry cleaning.
- **Make a sandwich** – The average office worker spends £3.30 on lunch each day, not to mention the coffees and afternoon snacks. Lunch and hot drinks from the kitchen at home cost a fraction of this, reduce packaging waste and increase the opportunity to avoid food waste.
- **Enjoy your job** – Without the distraction of a busy office, most home workers increase productivity and job satisfaction.
- **Save your car** – For car commuters working from home, there are further

savings in reduced wear and tear of the vehicle. Lower mileage means less frequent servicing and tyre replacement and less wear on engine parts. You could also consider car pooling rather than keeping your own car. There are time savings too in cutting out the commute.

Utilising technology

The availability of email and the internet, as well as communications technology such as video conferencing, webcams and conference calling has made home working much easier by facilitating contact with colleagues and clients.

- **Video conferencing** – Reduces travel to meetings and maintains face-to-face contact. Set up a webcam if your computer doesn't have a built-in camera.

- **Consolidate** – Use multi-purpose equipment such as a combined printer, copier and fax machine.

£ Know your rights

Self-employed home workers can claim enhanced capital allowances and offset the cost of energy-saving equipment against tax.

TOP TIPS FOR ENERGY EFFICIENCY

1. Be print and paper conscious – use recycled paper and don't print unless you have to.
2. Don't leave lights on in rooms that are not being used.
3. In summer, open the windows – don't use air conditioning or an electric fan.
4. Wear warm clothes in winter and heat only the room you are working in – not the whole house.
5. Improve the air quality of your home office with house plants.
6. Use a solar-powered calculator and clock.
7. Choose energy-recommended equipment with an A star energy rating.
8. Maintain a paperless office and archive digital documents on a disk.
9. Don't travel unless you have to – video conferencing gives face-to-face contact.
10. Recycle your print cartridges or use ones that are recycled or can be refilled.

INDEX

USEFUL WEBSITES

GENERAL

Computer Aid (www.computeraid.org) – For the recycling of computers, printer cartridges and mobile phones.

Directgov (http://actonco2.direct.gov.uk) – Includes a carbon footprint calculator.

Energy Saving Trust (www.energysavingtrust.org.uk) – Includes advice on energy-saving products, home improvements and generating your own electricity (including information about available grants).

Ethical Consumer Research Association (www.ethicalconsumer.org) – Free buyers' guides on numerous subjects including food and drink, health and beauty, money and technology.

Freecycle (www.freecycle.org) – An online recycling network which works on a local basis.

Waste and Resources Action Programme (www.wrap.org.uk) – Advice for individuals, businesses and local authorities on reducing waste and recycling more.

Women's Environmental Network (www.wen.org.uk) – Has information on subjects such as health, food and nappies.

HOME

Boiler Efficiency Database (www.boilers.org.uk) – To rate the efficiency of your boiler.

Green Electricity Marketplace (www.greenelectricity.org) – To find a green energy supplier.

Mercury Recycling (www.mercuryrecycling.co.uk) – Information on recycling anything containing mercury.

Recoup (www.recoup.org) – For information on plastics packaging recycling.

recycle-more (www.recycle-more.co.uk) – Advice on recycling at home, in school and in the workplace.

Recycling Appeal (www.recyclingappeal.com) – For recycling mobile phones, PDAs and printer cartridges.

uSwitch (www.uswitch.com) – To find your cheapest energy supplier.

Waste and Resources Action Programme (www.recyclenow.com) – Information on recycling and home composting.

GARDEN

National Society of Allotments and Leisure Gardeners (www.nsalg.org.uk) – To find your nearest allotment.

Timber Decking Association (www.tda.org.uk) – For information on decking from sustainable sources.

Waterwise (www.waterwise.org.uk) – For advice on reducing water consumption.

TRAVEL

The AA (www.theAA.com) – Includes a comprehensive route planner and traffic news.

Association of Independent Tour Operators (www.aito.co.uk) – To find specialist tour operators who adhere to sustainable tourism guidelines.

Carbon Balanced (www.carbonbalanced.org) – Carbon offsetting run by the UK-based charity World Land Trust.

Carplus (www.carclubs.org.uk) – To find details of your nearest car club.

International Ecotourism Society (www.ecotourism.org) – With members in over 90 countries, promotes the principles of eco-tourism and responsible travel.

LowFlyZone (www.lowflyzone.org) – To take a no-fly pledge.

The Man in Seat Sixty-One (www.seat61.com) – For advice on how to get almost anywhere by train and boat.

National Rail Enquiries (www.nationalrail.co.uk) – To plan your train journey in the UK.

Society of Motor Manufacturers and Traders (www.smmt.co.uk) – Database of CO_2 emissions for all cars registered since 1997.

Sustrans (www.sustrans.org) – The UK's leading sustainable transport charity.

Transport Direct (www.transportdirect.info) – For travel advice, including a carbon footprint calculator for your journey.

liftshare (www.liftshare.com/uk) – A national lift-sharing organistion.

Vehicle Certification Agency (www.vcacarfueldata.org.uk) – Database of the fuel efficiency of different cars.

Voluntary Carbon Standard (VCS) (www.v-c-s.org) – For accreditation of carbon offsetting schemes.

USEFUL WEBSITES CONTINUED

SHOPPING

Boxscheme Green & Organic Directory (www.boxscheme.org) – For details of organic box schemes.

Food Standards Agency (www.eatwell.gov.uk) – For information on storing food.

National Farmers' Retail & Markets Association (www.farmersmarkets.net) – To find your local farmers' market.

UK Police Property Disposal (www.bumblebeeauctions.co.uk) – For information on police auctions.

Waste and Resources Action (www.lovefoodhatewaste.com) – For tips on cutting food waste.

FINANCE

Ethical Investment Association (www.ethicalinvestment.org.uk) – For advice on ethical investments.

Ethical Investment Research Service (www.eiris.org) – To find a financial adviser specialising in ethical finance.

FAMILY

British Humanist Association (www.humanism.org.uk) – For information on spiritual but non-religious funerals.

National Association of Toy and Leisure Libraries (www.natll.org.uk) – To find your local toy library.

The Natural Death Centre (www.naturaldeath.org.uk) – For information on green funerals.

Women's Environmental Network (www.realnappiesforlondon.org.uk) – Information on real (cloth) nappies including a scheme for the exchange of cloth nappies and other equipment.

The Woodland Trust (www.woodland-trust.org.uk) – For information on recycling Christmas cards.

WORKPLACE

Carbon Trust (www.carbontrust.co.uk) – Energy-saving advice for businesses, including a carbon footprint calculator.

Department for Business Enterprise and Regulatory Reform (www.lowcarbonbuildings.org.uk) – For information on grants for businesses implementing major energy reductions.

Envirowise (www.envirowise.gov.uk) – The government-funded free advisory service on sustainable and profitable business practice.

ACKNOWLEDGEMENTS

The Automobile Association would like to thank the following photographers, companies and picture libraries for their assistance in the preparation of this book.

Abbreviations for the picture credits are as follows: (t) top; (b) bottom; (l) left; (r) right; (AA) AA World Travel Library.

3 © Clearview/Alamy; 4 RecycleNow Partners Photo Library; 6 RecycleNow Partners Photo Library; 6/7 RecycleNow Partners Photo Library; 7 RecycleNow Partners Photo Library; 8 Ecoscene / Alan Towse; 11bg © Adrian Sherratt/Alamy; 11 AA/T Mackie; 13 Thermafleece courtesy of Second Nature UK Ltd; 15 AA/S Montgomery; 16 Ecoscene/Sally Morgan; 17 RecycleNow Partners Photo Library; 19 Stockbyte Royalty Free; 20 AA/S Montgomery; 23 Royalty Free Photodisc; 24t RecycleNow Partners Photo Library; 24b AA/S Montgomery; 26 AA/J Tims; 29 AA/K Paterson; 30 Photolibrary Group; 33 AA/J Tims; 33bg AA/J Tims; 35; RecycleNow Partners Photo Library; 37 RecycleNow Partners Photo Library; 38 AA/M Moody; 41 AA/N Setchfield; 43 AA; 45 © imagebroker/Alamy; 47 AA/J Miller; 49 AA/A Mockford & N Bonetti; 50 AA/N Hicks; 53t Bananastock; 53b AA/S Montgomery; 55 AA/S Montgomery; 57 AA/S Montgomery; 59 RecycleNow Partners Photo Library; 60 AA/S Montgomery; 63 AA/J Tims; 65 OWL courtesy of 2 Save Energy plc; 67 © Jacques Jangoux/Alamy; 68 AA; 71 © Niall McDiarmid/Alamy; 73 AA/S Montgomery; 75 AA/S Montgomery; 76 RecycleNow Partners Photo Library; 79 AA/S Montgomery; 81 Willow Cromer coffin courtesy of Ecoffins; 82 © Jan Caudron/Anaklasis/Alamy; 85 RecycleNow Partners Photo Library; 87bg RecycleNow Partners Photo Library; 87 AA; 89 AA/S Montgomery; 90 AA/S Montgomery; 93 Stockbyte Royalty Free.

Every effort has been made to trace the copyright holders, and we apologise in advance for any accidental errors. We would be happy to apply any corrections in the following edition of this publication.